CW00420174

CONSISTENT CASH FLOW

CONSISTENT CASH FLOW

How to Get It, Track It and Keep It in Your Business

written by
Tom Palzewicz

foreword by **Bradley J. Sugars**

Please note that much of this publication is based on personal experience and anecdotal evidence. Although the authors and publisher have made every reasonable attempt to achieve complete accuracy of the content in the book, they assume no responsibility for errors or omissions. Also, you should use this information as you see fit, and at your own risk. Your particular situation may not be exactly suited to examples illustrated here; in fact, it is likely that they are not the same, and you should adjust your use of the imformation and recommendations accordingly.

Any trademarks, service marks, product names or named features are assumed to be the property of their respective owners, and are used only for reference. There is no implied endorsement if we use one of these terms.

DISCLAIMER: The contents of this Book are intended for the general information purpose only. Information contained in this document is not intended to be subsitute for legal advice or to provide legal guidance of any kind whatsoever. If legal advice or other expert assistance is required, the services of a competent professional should be sought.

Printed in the United States of America
First Printing: 2014

Library of Congress Control Number:
13-digit ISBN: 978-0-9884261-4-6

Book design by Scott Hooper

I would like to thank the hundreds of clients and businesses owners who've learned and mastered the elements of Consistent Cash Flow for providing feedback, encouragement and constructive criticism over the last eight years. You are the ones that helped me to create this book.

I would also like to thank my wife Terri and my children Max, Erik and Maddie for holding me accountable to my word, along with much needed editing. You are more helpful than you can possibly know.

Foreword

When it comes to your business, do you know how to keep score? One of the biggest problems business owners face is that they aren't sure of where their resources go and how they can do a better job utilizing those resources.

At ActionCOACH we call it "keeping score". Every business and business owner must "keep score" to know exactly where their resources are going and how to find more money and more time. Unfortunately many of these same business owners are stuck running their business on a day-to-day basis and don't have the time or energy to keep score in a productive way.

Even worse, myriad business owners are unsure of what to keep score on and how to measure all the important numbers in their business. In fact, this happens more often than you might think because most business owners never actually learned how to run a business.

The author of this book, Tom Palzewicz has made a career in helping business owners with just this challenge. As an ActionCOACH Business Coach, Tom has been extensively trained in our system and over his years working with business owners, he has found this to be one of the biggest challenges facing business owners today.

In his experience just understanding a company's financials and how to keep score, can make the difference between a struggling business and a business that thrives.

Numbers are the language of business and without proper understanding and management, your business won't last.

Tom has seen this scenario all too many times and has helped many business owners avoid this pitfall. While this is an indictment on the state of mind of many business owners, it is also incredibly beneficial to you, the reader. You see, Tom has seen it all when it comes to understanding a business' financials and he's taken that experience and distilled it into this book.

No stone has been left unturned in this book. Tom goes deep to bring you every aspect of "keeping score" in your business that you could possibly think of... and most importantly, he tells you why these areas are so important to your business and how you can utilize all of this reporting to build a business you can pass down to your children, or sell at a nice profit, some day.
Tom starts with the most important aspect of making any change, the mindset. Without proper mindset, changing is virtually impossible. And once you understand where your brain needs to be, Tom lets loose with terrific strategies and methodologies you will want to take to your business and begin putting to use right away.

Not only will you gain the ability to measure your numbers, you'll also develop the skills to forecast your financials, making planning and preparation that much more impactful and cost-effective.

So if you aren't sure how to keep score in your business, or even what you should be keeping score on, you've come to the right place. Get ready to learn strategies that will make your business better and last longer ...

Brad Sugars

Brad Sugars,
Founder and Chairman of ActionCOACH

Contents

CONSISTENT CASH FLOW

This book is **YOURS** with the compliments of

ActionCOACH Gary Wagstaff

If you need some help along the way,
just call me on **07793 714 995**

garywagstaff@actioncoach.com

INTRODUCTION

Running a business can be a rewarding and exhilarating experience. Delivering a product or service that fills a void or leaves a customer with pure delight is a challenging endeavor. Putting the ideas together and getting them on paper, creating a business plan, calculating projected profit and determining how to find people to make it all happen can make your head spin.

Getting started requires long hours and hard work. You have to keep an eye on each and every dollar to make sure your investment is paying off. Keeping track of all the details and persisting in the face of adversity is what all business owners go through until that moment when there seems to be just enough momentum that the flywheel starts to move. That's when the fun starts.

As they say in the opening ceremonies of the Olympics "Let the games begin". That is exactly what you have at this point, a game. Think of how you play most games, there is usually a set of rules complete with the directions on how to keep score. In order to know if you are winning the game you have to know how to keep score. All games have a well-defined point where a winner is declared.

Think of any professional sports team that you follow. They keep statistics on every player and timeframe to know exactly how not only the team is doing but each and every player on the field. Players know exactly where they stand and obsess with how to improve their numbers because they know that if they can increase their results, more money will follow.

Most business owners think they know the score by looking at their checkbook. If there is money in the bank, life is good. If the account is drained, time to worry. What if you ran your business like a sports team? What if you knew not only how well the team was doing but each member of your team? If a player is not performing, they are let go or demoted and someone else gets a chance to fill the role. The superstars are compared to previous ones and their numbers are subject to great scrutiny. The great ones are always in pursuit of a personal best.

What this book will show you is that your checkbook is the last piece of a long line of information that you have direct control over. Measuring each and every one of these pieces of information will help you to manage your business with more confidence and truly get what you need from your hard work. It will also help you understand what areas of your business you need to focus on, who your top performers are and who on your team needs some additional coaching and mentoring.

There is a saying in business that applies to numbers – "You can't manage what you don't measure". If you are like most business owners and you are looking to grow your business, where do you start? Knowing your numbers allows you to pinpoint the areas of your business that need the most attention and also allows you to "do the math" to determine how much you need to invest to make it grow.

Measuring the numbers needs to be done daily. The reason for this is actually quite simple. If you are truly committed to turning your dreams a reality, you need to do the right things every day. In order to be confident that you are doing the right things every day you need to start with Why. Why are you doing what you are doing? What's in it for you? What's in it for others? How do you figure that out? It all starts on the clarity of your Dreams.

There is a formula that you can use to help yourself understand the importance of this idea. Here is what it looks like:

D x **G** x **P** x **A**

Dreams x Goals x Plan x Action

This is what we call the formula for success. The "Why" is your Dreams. Think of the times you jump out of bed full of energy and enthusiasm for the day ahead. Are you clear on your purpose? Do you understand the results you choose to get and why they are important to you? Do you accomplish more with this pinpoint purpose? Of course you do. So what is a Dream?

A Dream is simply something that you choose to have, do or become combined with the lack of knowledge of how to make it happen. Martin Luther King, Jr. did not famously say "I have a plan" he said "I have a Dream". His personal vision struck a chord in people who were like minded and shared his vision. Once his dream was verbalized, momentum was created. "Why" are your Dreams?

Once you are clear on your Dreams, those Dreams need to be translated into Goals. This can be difficult for some people to do. How many times have you thought of goals or even taken the step to write them down only to put them in a drawer and forget about them. Sometimes even keeping a goal in front of us, say on the refrigerator door, has not helped us to accomplish them. What if your goals were SMART? Specific, Measurable, Achievable, Results Oriented and have a specific Timeframe, SMART. Your goals are represented by "What" you would choose to occur. "What" are your Goals?

Creating a concrete plan to achieve your goals is the next step in the process. Action plans are the most underutilized area of business. To paraphrase General Eisenhower, "planning is essential, plans are worthless". The sheer act of planning helps create awareness to potential situations and also begins to create an expectation that any challenge can be overcome with the right action. The plan then represents the "How". "How" is your Plan?

Once you have clarity around your Dreams, Goals and Plans, now you can determine what you need to do on a daily basis to turn these Dreams into reality. Your daily activity or action is the ultimate test and measure when it comes to your business. When you know the first three components of the formula, what you need to do every day becomes clearer. The actions you take are represented by the "When". "When" is your Action?

When you are able to create clarity of dreams it allows you to create meaningful goals. When you have meaningful goals it allows you to create a very detailed plan. When you have a detailed plan for success, you now know what the most important things are that need to be done every single day.
Why, What, How and When. Answering these questions, creating alignment and taking action will determine your level of success.

Let's give the formula a try. Rate yourself in each one of these categories –

with 10 being the highest and 1 being the lowest. How clear are you on your dreams? Do your goals align to your dreams? Does your plan show you reaching your goals? Does your daily calendar and that of your team allow everyone to stay on plan? Go ahead; fill in your numbers;

D (____) x **G** (____) x **P** (____) x **A** (____)

What is your score? The best possible score is 10,000 (10x10x10x10). Take your score and divide it by 10,000. Turn it into a percentage. Here is an example. Let's say that you are somewhat clear on your ultimate dreams – say a 4. You do set goals on a regular basis but struggle to achieve them – say a 5. You take the time to plan every year but not every quarter – a 6 and you feel like you are fighting fires every day – a 3.

D (4) x **G** (5) x **P** (6) x **A** (3)

Your score is (4x5x6x3) = 360. 360/10,000 = .036 or 3.6%. That is to say that you are living your life at less than 4% of capacity. From an optimistic point of view that means lots of room for improvement!

Imagine if you decided that every 90 days you were committed to increasing your score by one in each area. If you worked on it and moved each one up by 1 in the next 90 days, here is the new result.

D (5) x **G** (6) x **P** (7) x **A** (4)

(5x6x7x4) = 810. 810/10,000 = .081 or 8.1%. More than double the previous score!

Knowing what needs to happen every day in your business creates clarity of measurement. If you know what to measure, you will certainly be able to figure out how to measure it. When you start engaging your team in the measurement process, competition takes over and the results grow. When the results grow, there is more profit for you the business owner and therefore more money that you can use to incentivize your team toward even greater results. The business and the team are now aligned to focus on results. Imagine what your score could grow to if you actually focused on each of these elements.

If this sounds like the kind of business you would like to have, then this book will definitely help you get started. No matter what your education level and familiarity with accounting, this book will take you step by step through the process of putting a solid measurement system in place that will help you grow your business and ultimately achieve your dreams.

The systems and formulas presented in this book are intellectual property of ActionCOACH, IPCO Ltd.

HOW TO USE THIS BOOK

This book is divided into many different parts to help you make the transition from one step to the next. Start at the beginning and work your way through the exercises as each section will build on the previous sections. We will start with how you look at money including some definitions and beliefs around money in general. We will discuss the different pieces of financial reporting including your balance sheet and income and cash flow statements.

For some business owners, this book will seem very simple, for others complex. This book is not meant to be an Accounting or Financial Theory text book rather a practical set of easy to follow ideas to better run your business. Pick and choose what you will. If there is a particular subject you would like more information on, there are plenty of books to take you to the next level.

We will cover the Rule of Threes when it comes to financial statements to help you better understand your accountant and we will share some tools with you to help you create measurement systems and decision making tools to help you grow your business.

Then we will put it all together to help you create a dashboard that you can look at daily to make sure your business is on track. You will be able to put the checkbook away and pull out the numbers and then drift away to a worry free slumber knowing your business is allowing you to achieve your dreams.

Charlie

We begin by catching up with my mechanic Charlie, who has realized that he can no longer run his business from his checkbook. Now those who know him will be aware that he is no business tycoon. He doesn't have a mind for business numbers. But he will soon realize the need for measuring to help him manage and grow his business. Follow his experiences and learn as he did about the role measuring can play in business. You will discover, like he did, the power that measuring can have on your business and how it can turn your future around.

You might be surprised at how much each exercise will reveal about your business. It may get you thinking about important issues that have never crossed your mind before. If some of this information is new to you, don't be concerned. There's never been a better time to start working on your business.

Make sure you make notes along the way and fill in the information that the exercises require. You will learn much more by taking action on each and every area than just reading about it. You will find proven ideas that, when combined with your new knowledge, will bring results.

Now it's time to get started. There are customers out there waiting to deal with you and your team. All you need right now is a way to keep track of everything to help you know that you and your team are on track. And where will that leave you? With a predictable growing business that someday will work without you!

So grab a calculator, log on to your computer and let's get started!

Charlie Learns the Importance of Keeping Score!

My relationship with Charlie, my trusted mechanic, goes back a long way, He had been recommended by a friend when I bought my first sports car sixteen years ago, and I've always been more than happy with the work he has done for me since.

He came highly recommended and I can see why; his work is second to none, his prices are competitive, and he gives great customer service. He really is more than just a mechanic – he's a car enthusiast, as well.

But the more I got to know him, the more I realized that he knew very little about running a business. But to be fair to him, I'd have to say that he was no worse than most business owners I'd met. He knew how to do his job well. But this was where he was going wrong, because he actually owned the garage, he didn't just work there as one of the mechanics.

The more I had to do with the business, the more I could see that it wasn't reaching its full potential. In fact, it was nowhere near as successful as it should have been. You see, Charlie was spending all his time working in his business and not on it. Nobody was planning ahead, putting in place the building blocks that would take the business to the next level, and then the one after that.

What Charlie needed to learn was the attitude needed to prosper, the real functions of a business owner and the strategies involved in working on the five key areas of any business, what I call the Business Chassis. Here is how the Business Chassis or 5 Ways works in a business.

5 WAYS BUSINESS CHASSIS

Number of Leads

x

Conversion Rate

=

Customers

x

# of Transactions

x

Average $$$ Sale

=

Revenue

x

Profit Margins

=

Profit

As Charlie and I became friends, I began coaching him, and his eyes were opened! He told me he had no idea how off the mark he had been, as far as running a business is concerned. We started slowly, working on the last part of the chassis first. The final part of the Business Chassis, the margins, was perhaps the most illuminating for Charlie. You see, we were able to try things his inner self said he shouldn't, like increasing his prices by 10 percent. He really didn't want to do this, but I insisted. He was stunned when all it did was give him more profit. He didn't lose a single customer. In fact, none of them even noticed!

The next part of the Business Chassis that we worked on was the number of transactions his customers made. Just a small 10 percent increase here made a huge difference to his business, and his profit. After that we tackled his average dollar sale. This is the fourth part of the Business Chassis. Charlie was able to identify missed opportunities and implemented strategies aimed at correcting this, and increasing the average amount his customers spent when having their cars serviced at the same time. Charlie was truly amazed by what these strategies did for his business.

We then turned our attention to the next part of the Business Chassis, his conversion rate. That was a real eye-opener. Charlie had no idea that he actually had to convert his prospects into customers. He simply assumed it would just happen all by itself. He thought people who needed their cars serviced would become customers, if they thought the price was right. But I wasn't surprised. Most people seem to think the same way.

Now that we had the rest of the business set to grow we now turned to lead generation or marketing. Once he had begun receiving a steady flow of new leads, he now had a sense of predictability in his business.

All along the way Charlie had realized the power of measuring. When he knew his numbers he knew his business. He started to make business decisions based on facts instead of feelings and the results soon followed.

After having worked on the Business Chassis, Charlie's Garage started to become well known in his area. His customers began noticing the difference, not only in their whole experience visiting the workshop, but also because they could feel there was a buzz about the place. Charlie began extricating himself from the workshop and began to spend more time managing and directing. At first he felt strange in his new role, but after a while he began to really enjoy it. As he became comfortable working on the business, he began to become more adventurous. He also began thinking like a businessperson and not a mechanic.

The work Charlie did on his margins really got him thinking. He started to wonder what else he needed to know in order to get his cash flow to a consistently high level that would allow him to concentrate on other things. He was used to tracking his checking account every day and working out in his head if he would have enough money in the bank to make the next payroll. What if he could know how much cash his business was going to generate for the next six weeks or even three months? How much more confidence would he have to reinvest in his business? He often was tempted to borrow from the bank to expand though fear always stopped him from pulling the trigger. How could he pay back a loan if he often did not know if he could make payroll? Things seemed to be different now, but would it continue?

It was this that brought me to his office for another meeting.

"Good morning Charlie, nice to see you again," I said as I stepped into his office. There were always different engine parts and all sorts of kinds of furniture in his office, though he always pulled out the same chair for me to sit in. As usual, he sat back in his old tattered chair behind his cluttered desk.

"I am really glad to see you, I have been up all night bouncing something around in my head and I need to ask you something", Charlie said, surprising me with his directness. Charlie usually liked to discuss the latest addition to my extensive collection of fine cars, but not today. I could see that he wanted to get right to business, just like I do.

"Brad, the reason I asked you to drop by is there is something that I need to figure out, and I know you are the guy to ask. After implementing the business chassis and seeing my business really start to take off, I realized that I really need to track all sorts of things when it comes to money. I'm tired of waking up at night and thinking about payroll and parts and rent. It always seems to work out but I still worry about it all the same," Charlie said, clearly ready to now ask his question.

"Is there a way for me to track my cash flow that would allow me to sleep better at night"?

I could clearly see that Charlie was now ready to start running his business by the numbers. He had heard all about my investing in other business and real estate, and I knew this is where he wanted to get. Charlie wanted to know how to keep financial score of a business. And he wanted to know right away.

"Well Charlie, I am very glad to hear that question coming from you. You see, keeping score is the most important rule of business. Business is a game, and if you don't keep score, you never know if you are winning", I said. "In order to win, you have to know what the rules are. When you know the rules of winning, then you know what and to keep score. When you know what you need to track, then the rest falls into place. You see Charlie; each business has different things they need to track depending on the type of business. Some businesses sell stuff, others sell time. When you understand what type of business you have, you are ready to set up your scorecard".

Charlie thought to himself for a moment. You could see the wheels spinning in his head as he thought about his business. "Isn't that what I pay an accountant to do, keep score?" said Charlie. "I send him my bank statement and credit card statement and anything else he asks for and he sends me my reports and tells me what I owe for taxes. If there is anything left, I get to keep it", Charlie said. "Isn't that my scorecard?" He asked.

"I suppose it is Charlie", I said. "How often do you look at those reports?"

"Once a year", Charlie replied.

"How often are you tracking your business chassis numbers?" I said.

"Mostly weekly, sometimes monthly" Charlie replied. I let his reply hang in the air for a moment. I was almost blinded when the light bulb went on above his head. "You mean I need to look at my numbers more than once a year?" He gasped.

"What if you read your financial reports every month and knew your cash flow every week? What if you already knew what your reports were going to say because they just confirmed your daily scorecard?" I said.

"That would certainly help me sleep at night!" Charlie said, the impact of this conversation becoming clear to him.

I let him sit for a while and let the concept sink in. I could tell he had many questions running through his mind and he was just looking for the first one to ask.

"Brad, I have had an accountant ever since that day you told me in order to have a real business, I need to hire an accountant. You were right, it was a great investment and kept me from making some financial mistakes. I have to tell you though, half the time I don't know what he is talking about. I feel foolish asking him questions because I think I should already know this stuff." Charlie said.

"Charlie, join the club. I went to school for accounting and even then some things left me wondering how they were going to help me run my business." I said. "What I did instead was asked myself a lot of questions, and then built my own scorecard that helped me run my business instead of using what my accountant thought was the right thing."

"Brad, would you teach me how to do that for my business?" Charlie replied.

"I am glad you finally asked, Charlie. It would be my pleasure. But first, let's talk about your relationship with money!" I said.

PART 1

My Relationship with Money

One of the most important relationships you will have in life is your relationship with money. Your thoughts around money have the ability to hold you back or allow you to jump ahead of where you are now. There have been many books written on this subject, so if you have not done anything to help foster a great relationship with money, the best time to start is now.

The first thing to think about is how you look at your financial results. How many times have you said to yourself that the company could have done better if it weren't for the economy, problem customers, lack of funds for marketing, etc…? Time to start thinking above the line with your money before we can move forward.

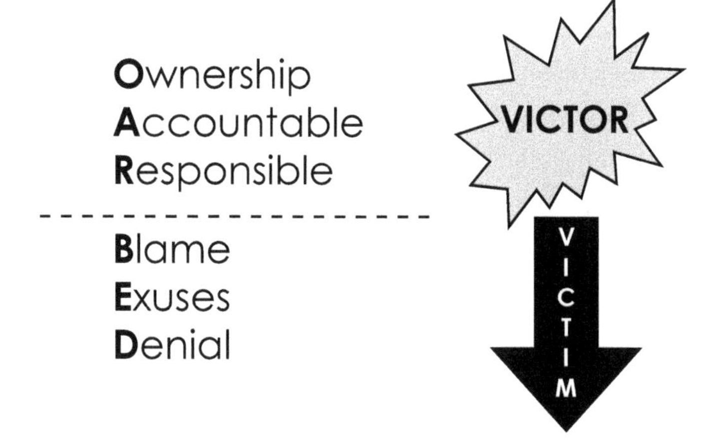

There is a line in life that decides our outcomes and results. This line is called the line of decision or the line of choice. Every single day, every single moment we have a choice to make; do we want to be a victim or a victor.

The victim mentality revolves around blame, excuses and denial. Business owners blame the economy, the government, banks, customers or anything else they can think of in order to not accept responsibility of their business. They use excuses like lack of sales, operational problems or lack of good employees to justify their financial position. Or they just put their head in the sand and continue to go broke because they do not want to make the hard choices or decisions that come with owning a business.

The below-the-line business is a reasons-based business. Everyone in the company will come up with a reason why things can't change and the business will slowly but surely go out of business. Doubt, fear and negativity are the emotions that rule the day in a victim-based business.

The above-the-line business is just the opposite, there is a focus on results; because results drive profitability and profitability drives cash flow.

When the business owner takes responsibility of the numbers, then the business has a chance to grow. When the team and the owner are willing to be held accountable to those results, then the business can move forward and when there is ownership of the numbers, the business will grow and thrive. What kind of business owner are you? Above-or-below-the-line? Victim or victor?

This one simple decision can mean the difference between success and failure. If you are the type of owner that consistently lives above-the-line, then keep reading this book. If you are not, then you have a decision to make. Are you ready to look in the mirror and tell yourself that everything that is right and wrong with your business is because of you? If the answer is no, then you might as well throw this book in the trash and move on. If the answer is yes, then it is time to take control of your business and life and get to the business of making money. Are you ready? Great! Let's move on then.

What we need to understand next is a simple definition of money. Here is our definition of money. See if you can make sense of it.

An idea backed by confidence plus action. Think about that for a minute. An idea backed by confidence plus action. Have you ever said to yourself that you don't have any money? A better question would be which one of these three

So, what is money ... ?

An idea backed by confidence plus action ...

pieces are you missing? Are you out of ideas? Have you created an action plan? Do you lack confidence?

All of these things are essential for money to exist. Each country has its own currency. Paper currency used to be backed by some hard currency (gold, silver, etc...). That is no longer the case. Most would agree that a $20 bill is worth twenty dollars. It is worth $20 because we believe in the idea that it is worth twenty dollars and there is a very high degree of confidence that it will be worth $20 tomorrow. The last part, an action plan, is derived from the fact that most governments are very good at collecting taxes to pay for services. Therefore, this action plan boosts our confidence in the value of the piece of paper.

Think about your business. Apply the definition back to yourself. Are you out of ideas to improve your business? How many ideas are you not doing anything with because you are just not getting to them? Do you lack confidence in those ideas? Do you have a system that helps you evaluate ideas? Do you have an action plan that you are following every day? If you answered yes to these three questions then most likely your business, and your cash flow or money are also growing. If this is not the case, then which part needs work? Before we move forward, decide which part of this definition is holding you back and then write down your next step.

Ideas: ....

Action Plan: ....

Confidence: ....

So what areas of our definition do you need to work on the most? Most business owners I know are rarely out of ideas. There is usually just a lack of time or team to implement them. Confidence usually increases as the plan is implemented and positive outcomes are realized.

Sometimes we are not aware of how our actions are actually keeping us from moving closer to our goals. Self-sabotage is a human condition with which we are all infected. Self-sabotage is usually a direct result of some limiting belief we hold about whatever it is we are attempting to create. Let's apply that rationale to money.

5 Beliefs you have about ...

MONEY?

Before we do an exercise to help you uncover some potential limiting beliefs, let's define what a belief is. A belief is something that you hold to be true. The difference between a belief and a fact is that facts are always true; beliefs may or may not be true. In the space below write down five beliefs you have around money.

1. ....
2. ....
3. ....
4. ....
5. ....

Next to each belief, put a plus sign (+) if you would think that belief is positive or helpful, a negative sign (-) if you think that belief is negative or no sign if you think it is a neutral belief. Add up the positive and negatives. How many of each do you have? If you have more positive than negative, what does that say about your relationship with money? If there are more negative than positive, how much are those negative beliefs holding you back?

Let me give you an example. A common belief is that money is the root of all evil. First we need to determine if this belief is positive or negative? Money can be used for both productive and destructive purposes. Most would agree that this belief is negative as money is a tool and the use of money will determine the outcome. So if your belief is that money is the root of all evil, how often will you work both consciously and subconsciously to push money (evil) away? Will you pull back in your business at the first sign of success? Will you give away your products or services because it would be greedy to make money from them? At the first sign of a healthy profit will you find an unimportant issue to focus on and slow down momentum?

Let's look at another common belief; I need to work hard to make money. We spoke about business momentum and the idea of a flywheel. Once there is enough force or push to get the flywheel going, there is synergy and things get easier. If your belief is that hard work equals money, then it will always be harder to grow your business, never easier. You will fear taking time off and letting others do things for you because they will not work as hard as you and the business will suffer. You will never truly leverage your business because leverage makes things easier.

Here is another formula that directly applies to beliefs;

Be x Do = Have

The ***Be*** is directly attributable to your thoughts and beliefs. The ***Do*** is your activity or action and the ***Have*** is the results you are able to drive through your business. In order to increase your results, or Have, one of the other components of the formula must change. Most business owners are already investing most of their time in their business so the one place with the largest room for improvement is the Be. By changing your Be, or your beliefs, your results will automatically improve.

Take a look at the beliefs you wrote down. How many are negative? Are you happy with your beliefs? Is it time to throw some of those beliefs out and create some new ones? If that is the case, then here is what we need to do next. What is the opposite of that belief that is holding you back? How could you phrase it in a powerful way to start turning that negative belief around?

Write the new improved belief here:

....

....

....

....

....

What would happen to your life if you adopted this new and improved belief? Is it worth investing time to change it? Only you can decide the answer to that question, but if your answer is yes, here is what you need to do next; Put that new belief in a place where you can see it on a regular basis. Say it to yourself several times a day. Keep saying it until that little voice in your head no longer laughs but agrees with the statement. It is at this point you should see some changes in your financial position for the better. If this is true, keep going, if not rework the statement and try again. Keep changing it until you see results!

Beliefs are habits, some are good for you and others are not. Keep the ones that work and change the ones that don't and start taking responsibility for your relationship with money and you will see a change in yourself and the people around you!

Here are some other thoughts on money before we move into the next topic. There is a major difference between Debt and Financial Leverage. Just so we can put the proper perspective on the previous statement, let's make sure of some definitions. Our definition of Debt is borrowing money without a plan of how to pay it back. Financial Leverage is using Other People's Money (OPM) to grow your business or your life. Most people confuse the two and end up accumulating debt and shying away from financial leverage.

Credit Cards, Accounts Payable and Lines of Credit are the most common ways that businesses accumulate debt. These short-term and expensive borrowing sources are easy tools to cover up bad decision making and rarely are coupled with a plan of how to pay back. There is usually just the hope that business will pick up or turn around, and as soon as that happens, the money will be paid back. Recognizing debt for what it is and then sitting down and creating a repayment plan will go a long way to getting out of debt. A good rule of thumb is to take the time period it took to accumulate the debt and use that same time to pay it off so as not to put undue pressure on current cash flow.

In a growing business, cash is essential to powerful growth. Using financial leverage or OPM in the right situations can help accelerate that growth. Banks love to lend money for stuff and things. They can use the stuff or things as collateral to get the loan approved. It is easier to get a loan to buy stuff than to fund other parts of the business. They can't use your people or brand as collateral. As long as the loan is paid off when the things are old or used up, financial leverage can significantly improve the growth rate of any business. We will explore this principle on a more detailed basis in Part 7.

One last thought on money. How many times in your life have you absolutely needed money and you somehow found a way to get it? Paying the rent or mortgage. Payroll. Helping out someone in need. This is not a coincidence. It is simply the work of a fundamental principle known as the Law of Vacuum. The Law of Vacuum states that nature abhors a vacuum. Where there is space, nature is working to fill it. This principle can be seen all the way from the expanding universe to that closet you just cleaned out. Empty space will be filled.

Given this principle, what does this have to do with money? Think back to the Formula we just walked through. When our Dreams get bigger, what happens to our Goals? Don't they grow? When we create space in our minds for what we would truly like to see come into our life, we are creating space. When we create space, the Law of Vacuum kicks in and begins to work to fill that space. Need is simply space that the universe fills.

So if this is true, how do we use this principle to allow us to grow our business? The first thing we need to do is create space. Dream Big. Set Goals that allow you to achieve your Dreams. It takes the same amount of time to plan big as it does to plan small. Fill your calendar with the right things and watch the results happen. Become aligned to your true intentions and it will become easier to keep your attention on what is truly important every day.

So now that you have learned how to create a mindset for success, let's jump into the details that are going to allow you to achieve that success financially. Just like with anything else, in order to master a subject we first must learn the language. Next up, learning to speak Accountant!

Review

Let's do a quick review of the main topics discussed in this chapter starting with ...

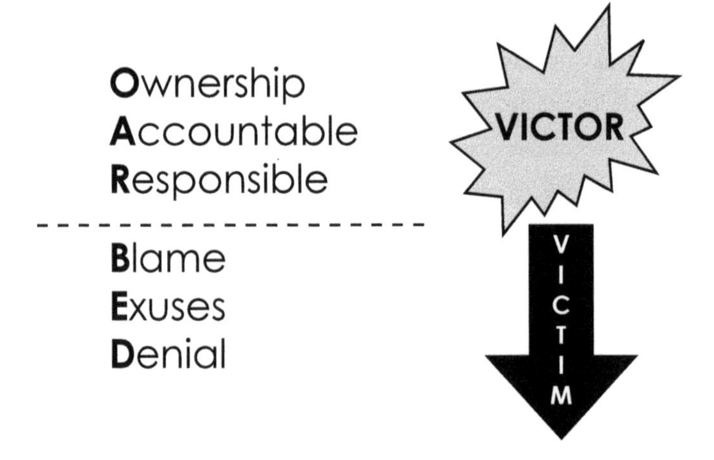

Remember, it starts with you. ***Dreams x Goals x Plan x Activity***. Are you taking responsibility for your business and your life or are you stuck below the line playing the victim?

So, what is money ... ?

An idea backed by confidence plus action ...

When you are testing and measuring everything in your business, action becomes easier and confidence rises as there is empirical proof that things do work. Confidence is the key. How much more confident will you be when you have put all of the ideas in this book into practice?

What are your beliefs around money and how many of them do you need to change?

5 Beliefs you have about ...

MONEY?

Be x Do = Have along with your beliefs around money need to be examined on a regular basis. Use the Law of Vacuum and OPM (other people's money) along with Financial Leverage coupled with the correct daily action will help you build your business faster!

PART 2

The Language of Numbers

Revenue, profit, equity, cash flow, assets, liabilities, cash or accrual basis, the lists goes on and on. How many times have you sat with your accountant and asked yourself "What are they talking about?" How many times have you not asked because it is your business and you are supposed to know these things? Why doesn't my accountant just tell me what I need to know?

The real question is what do you need to tell your accountant so that they can do a better job of helping you? Do you know what you need from them and when you need it? Do you understand your financial reports, how they are set up, what they tell you about the past and more importantly what they tell you about the future?

For most business owners, the answer to these questions are usually no. That is not to say that they don't understand some of the things they are looking at or what the numbers tell them about their business. What it does say is there is a general lack of understanding what the reports can do for you and how to use them to achieve your dreams. This lack of understanding starts with the language and the structure of the reports themselves.

Let's start with some basic language. If you think about any basic information system it starts with an index or set of assumptions or rules. This index in the language of accounting is known as the Chart of Accounts and the rules are known as GAAP or Generally Accepted Accounting Principles coupled with the Tax Laws of the area you do business in. The rules will dictate what information you are required to keep along with what other information you want to create. The index will determine how you view the information.

It is important to understand that there is no such thing as an Accounting Emergency. Everything you do in the world of accounting can be redone given enough time. Sure there are always time limits imposed on the rules we mentioned, though if you are on top of your data, there are always options to every situation. A good accountant understands this. This idea can be summed up in the following story;

A business owner is looking for a new accountant. He puts out an ad and three people answer it, an Engineer, a CPA (Certified Public Accountant) and a Controller with a lengthy work history. The owner decides to interview all three and ask only one question. The Engineer walks in and the owner invites him to sit down and asks him "What is 2 + 2?" the Engineer takes out his calculator, punches in the numbers, double checks his answer and confidently says "4, my answer is 4". The owner thanks him and sends him on his way. The CPA is next. The owner asks him "What is 2 +2?" He confidently says "4" and the owner sends him on his way. Finally the Controller walks in and the owner asks her the same question, "What is 2 + 2?" The Controller gets up, closes the door, leans over the table and whispers "What do you need it to be?" The owner immediately hires her.

It's not that the owner is trying to evade taxes or that the controller is trying to somehow game the system. It's that the controller understands that the numbers need to work for the owner, not the other way around. The more you understand the rules of the game, the easier it is to win the game.

MASTERY level business owners wear ...

... in relationship to money

So let's start by describing the different pieces of money and who creates or is responsible for them and why they are important. There are four main parts to money in any business:

1. **Revenue**
2. **Profit**
3. **Flow**
4. **Equity**

Let's start with ***Revenue.***

1. **Revenue**

EMPLOYEE

Money paid for doing the job ...

Employees are responsible for generating revenue. As stated above, it is the money paid for doing a job. Revenue is probably the easiest element of money to track in the business. There are usually goals set up tied to revenue throughout the business. You are wearing the Employee hat in your business when you are creating Revenue.

Next up is ***Profit***.

2. **Profit**

Money left after expenses ...

Profit is what is left over after paying expenses. There are two types of profit; Gross Profit and Net Profit. Gross Profit is what is left over after paying your variable costs, while Net Profit is what is left over after paying for expenses. It is up to the manager to make sure that there is money left over after paying all of the bills. You are wearing the Manager hat in your business when you are creating profit.

Next up is ***Cash Flow***.

3. **Flow**

OWNER

Money moving through the business ...

Cash Flow is money moving through the business. Money in, money out. Some businesses have very little money moving through the business, some have enormous amounts. It is the Owner's responsibility to make sure that the business has enough cash to meet their needs. Some businesses are very profitable yet cannot grow because there is not enough cash to support the growth. You are wearing the Owner hat in your business when you are tracking Cash Flow.

And the last hat is ***Equity***.

4. **Equity**

Money-value of the business itself ...

Equity represents the actual dollar value of the business itself. Now each of these hats represents a different form that money takes in the business. Therefore each of these hats needs some kind of financial scorecard to help understand if we are winning or losing the game. You are wearing the Investor hat in your business when you are determining Equity.

So which hat are you wearing in your business? How much time do you spend wearing the revenue hat? Profit hat? Cash flow hat? Equity hat? Most business owners are usually wearing all of these hats at some point in the business. The first two hats can be delegated to the team as most business owners hire someone to generate revenue and manage the books. The third hat can also be delegated to the right person but needs to be verified by some outside source while the last hat is the reason to own a business as we will see further in the book.

It is important to understand each of these pieces of money in your business and who is responsible for the creation and tracking of each type. As the business owner, you are responsible for tracking the four different components of money and in order to track we need to start with our index or in accounting language a Chart of Accounts.

The Chart of Accounts is simply the backbone of your accounting system.

Every entry, invoice, expense and report will use this index. Therefore you need to make some simple decisions when it is time to set up your Chart of Accounts.

Glossary of Financial Terms

1. Chart of Accounts
   a) List of all the account titles in a general ledger
   b) Grouped by assets, liabilities, equity, revenues and expenses
2. Cash vs. Accrual Basis *(accounting methods that determine how to record income and expenses)*
   a) **Cash Basis** — Income and expenses are recorded when money is received or disbursed
   b) **Accrual Basis** — Income and expenses are recorded when they have occurred

From a summary perspective, here are the categories that make up the detail:

1000–1999: asset accounts
2000–2999: liability accounts
3000–3999: equity accounts
4000–4999: revenue accounts
5000–5999: cost of goods sold or cost of sales
6000–6999: expense accounts or fixed costs
7000–7999: other revenue (for example, interest income)
8000–8999: other expense (for example, income taxes)

Now let's look at a sample of the detail;

Current Assets

1000 Cash
1020 Accounts Receivable
1040 Inventory

Property, Plant & Equipment

1100 Equipment
1101 Accumulated Depreciation - Equipment
1110 Equipment – Office
1111 Accumulated Depreciation – Office Equipment
1120 Leasehold Improvements
1121 Accumulated Amortization – Leasehold Improvements

Other Assets

1500 Deposits

Current Liabilities

2000 Line of Credit
2010 Accounts Payable
2030 Accrued Wages and Payroll Taxes Withheld

Long Term Liabilities

2100 Notes Payable

Equity

3000 Common Stock
3100 Retained Earnings

Revenue

4000 Commercial Sales
4010 Residential Sales
4020 Other Sales

Direct Costs

5000 Direct Labor
5100 Sub-Contractors
5200 Equipment
5300 Materials and Supplies
5400 Travel
5500 Other/Miscellaneous
5610 Vacation
5615 Holidays
5620 Sick Leave
5625 Payroll Taxes
5630 401(k) Plan
5635 Group Insurance

Overhead Costs

6000 Other Labor
6110 Amortization - Leasehold Improvements
6120 Depreciation - Lab Equipment
6130 Depreciation - Office Equipment
6140 Rent
6150 Utilities
6160 Telephone
6170 Equipment Rental
6180 Expendable Equipment
6190 Repairs & Maintenance
6200 Office Supplies
6210 Travel
6220 Consultants
6230 Dues & Subscriptions
6240 Training
6330 Licenses

This Chart of Accounts is the beginning point of the reporting system. The Account Numbers are used to help create a hierarchy that the system can use to produce reports with meaningful sub-total and totals. As you can see these areas are grouped by Assets, Liabilities, Equity, Revenue and Expenses.

The above is just a sample. There are an unlimited number of accounts you can set up in your system. It is very important to understand what you want to measure since this will help you decide what accounts you choose to set up. If you are going to measure it, create a place or account for it. Remember, if you can measure it you can manage it!

We will be referencing this Chart of Accounts throughout the rest of Part 2. Please go back and take a look at the example so that you can start to understand the different pieces that each of your financial reports are going to use. Look at the categories and think about how each of the examples in each category applies to your business.

If you are already using a Chart of Accounts take a look at each area and determine if you have the right categories for your business. Is there enough detail? Is there too much detail in some areas? If you are not using some accounts, get rid of them. Did you add a new type of business recently? Do you have an expense that is lumped into another category that is now growing and needs a line of its own? If you think you need more detail in some areas, add them now is the time to change it before moving on in this book.

The next topic we need to cover is Cash versus Accrual based accounting. As shown on page 24, these are different accounting methods that determine how to record income and expenses.

Cash Basis - Income and expenses are recorded when money is received or disbursed

Accrual Basis - Income and expenses are recorded when they have occurred

Most companies use Accrual based accounting simply because it allows the business owner to match revenue and expenses in the same period to give a better representation of profit. Remember though, profit is not cash. You cannot buy groceries, pay the mortgage or your other bills with profit. Cash basis will help you understand where your cash went, but a better report is your Statement of Cash Flows that we will discuss in Part 4.

So now that we have a chart of accounts, we need to take a look at what reports we are going to need on a consistent basis to be able to determine the scorecard for our business. Let's start at the top of the Chart of Accounts and work our way down. The first accounts in our overall list have to do with the Balance Sheet.

Glossary of Financial Terms

1. Balance Sheet
   a) Shows the financial position of a company at a particular point in time
   b) Allows the reader to view the total resources of the company and determine how the assets are being financed
   c) Is a record of the liquidity of the business and the owner's equity at a given point in time
   d) It's a snapshot of the business that shows what the business owns and what the business owes
2. Assets
   a) What is owned by the company: cash, accounts receivable, inventories and plant and equipment; recorded at acquisition price

3. Liabilities
   a) What the company owes: accounts payable, loans, credit card balances and unpaid sales and payroll taxes
4. Owner Equity
   a) The difference between what you have and what you owe

As you can see from the information above, the Balance Sheet allows the reader to view the total resources of the company and how they are being financed. It is broken into Assets, which is what you own, and Liabilities, which is what you owe and Equity which is the difference between the two. It is important to note that the Balance sheet is only good for a particular point in time. Think of it like a snapshot of your business, once you take the picture things start to change. The important thing to understand about the Balance Sheet is that you need to consistently take the snapshot and then understand the differences in the picture.

The Balance Sheet is normally run at the end of a period, say month end or quarter end and your Tax Accountant will need the year-end balance sheet. The day after you run the report the Balance Sheet will have changed due to the fact that your business changes.

Assets are broken up into three different categories; Short term, long term and other. Liabilities are broken up into the same three categories; Short term, long term and other.

Converting this into the Chart of Accounts looks like this:

1000–1999: asset accounts
2000–2999: liability accounts
3000–3999: equity accounts

So to summarize, the Balance Sheet is where you keep track of what you own and what you owe and it shows the difference between the two. Keeping track of your assets is the first step in being able to determine if you are getting an expected rate of return on them. Tracking your liabilities helps you understand how to look at your predicted payback period when you use yours or other people's money to grow the business. Finally tracking your equity will help you determine when it is appropriate to take your returns out of your business or look for investors to grow. We will discuss the Balance Sheet in much greater detail in Part 5.

Now let's move on to the Income Statement. The Income Statement, also known as the Profit and Loss Statement or the P&L, is the tracking mechanism to determine if the company is making a profit.

Glossary of Financial Terms

1. Income Statement / Profit Loss Statement
   a) List the revenues and expenses
   b) Shows the results of operations for a period of time: monthly, quarterly and annually
2. Fixed Costs
   a) Costs that do not change in total as business activity increases or decreases. Examples include rent, property insurance and property taxes
3. Variable Costs
   a) Costs that increase in total proportionately with an increase in activy decreases proportionately with a decrease in activity. Examples include direct materials, direct labor and utilities

As you can see, just like the Balance Sheet the Income Statement is made up of three parts; Revenue (Sales, Income), Expenses (Fixed and Variable) and Profit (or Loss). Unlike the Balance Sheet the Income Statement is run for a particular period of time. An Income Statement can be run for a day, week, month, quarter, year or any period you would like.

Converting this into the Chart of Accounts looks like this:

4000–4999: revenue accounts
5000–5999: cost of goods sold or cost of sales
6000–6999: expense accounts or fixed costs
7000–7999: other revenue *(for example, interest income)*
8000–8999: other expense *(for example, income taxes)*

The idea behind the Income Statement is that you want to be able to determine if your income from revenue generating activity is greater than the costs associated with producing that revenue for a particular period of time.

Revenue can be broken into as many categories as you choose. It is important to note that if you are going to focus on a product or service it would be wise to set up an account to track the revenue. This also holds true for any costs associated with generating that revenue. You should also set up your variable cost accounts to be able to track the product or service just like revenue. Variable costs, otherwise known as Cost of Goods Sold (COGS) or Cost of Sales (COS) are important in the determination of pricing and Gross Profit.

In addition, you will need to set up different accounts to track your fixed expenses. In order to control your fixed expenses, you will need a way to track them and be able to understand if you are making enough money to cover all of your expenses in order to make a profit. The Income Statement is your tool that will help you figure that out. We will discuss this in much greater detail with many examples in the next section, Part 3.

The Income Statement can be run for any period of time though the most common period for looking at an Income Statement is monthly. Why monthly, you ask? One of the interesting things we have decided as human beings is that we like to pay for stuff over periods of time. When we buy something big or even rent something big we like to break up payments over some time period. Paying annually can be difficult on cash flow. Paying quarterly can also be difficult on cash flow, though significantly more manageable. Daily would be ridiculous, though there are some people that do buy the same things every day like coffee or food.

Most of us like to pay for things monthly. Think of most of your fixed costs. You pay them monthly. Rent, utilities and vehicles are great examples of these kinds of expenses. Therefore most business owners look at their monthly P&L so they can determine if they made any money that month. We will cover why this is true in Part 3 when we discuss Break Even.

It is important to understand that we are talking about Financial Reporting. There are two distinct kinds of financial reporting, GAAP and Management reporting. As we mentioned before, GAAP or Generally Accepted Accounting Principles are used to help companies report their financial information with a level of consistency across all industries. Large companies produce complex end of year books that contain their financial reports along with other information to help their shareholders understand their investment. Financial regulators take great care to ensure shareholders have the best information possible to make decisions about their investments.

This is great in large companies with multiple shareholders, but what about the business with relatively few shareholders comprised of the owner and maybe some family or other partners? These businesses need their financial reports to help them understand if their business plan and activities are allowing them to produce the cash flow to achieve the goals tied to their dreams. They need something more.

Larger companies understand this and have taken the time to create management reports that are not constrained by GAAP. These reports are created outside of the context of GAAP and are used to run the business on a daily basis. There may even be other systems outside of the Chart of Accounts that are used to keep track of pertinent information used to run the business.

Here is the rub; your accountant is tasked with helping you comply with your local tax code, and supplying information back to your banker and making sure your Statements comply with GAAP. You need management reports that help you understand if you are achieving your goals. These two competing needs most times collide.

This is where you need to work with your accountant to translate your needs into some reporting structure that will allow both of you to satisfy the wants. At the end of this book we are going to help you come up with a plan to approach your accountant to have them help you with your management reporting needs. They will be excited to help and you will get your reports faster than if you try to do it yourself. Win-Win.

Now that we have dived into some of the language of accountancy and the reason behind it, the Chart of Accounts, Balance Sheet and Income Statement or P&L, it is time to move on and start defining how to create the right information to use in running your business. So be patient and get ready to learn the how to really keep score to allow you to achieve your dreams!

Review

How many hats are you wearing in your business?

Which ones do you need to delegate? Which ones do you need to keep? Are you willing to do what it takes to have a "Commercial, Profitable Business that Works without You"?

Do you have your Chart of Accounts set up in your Accounting System? Have you decided what you need your financial reports to look like and what information you would like from them on a consistent basis?

Are you clear on your financial terms? At the end of each section in this book there is a list of terms. Review them consistently until you understand the language of accounting.

Do you understand the difference between accounting and financial reporting? Is your accountant expecting you to run your business through their reports or your reports?

MASTERY level business owners wear ...

... in relationship to money

PART 3

The P&L, Break Even Formula and the Rule of 3's

This part of the book will work to help you understand the first two money hats in business, Revenue and Profits. These are the most important hats in your business because if there are no sales, there is no business. If there is no profit, the business will not survive. You have heard the statistic before, 80% of all businesses fail in the first five years, another 80% of those fail in the second five years. Most businesses fail due to a lack of cash flow. Lack of cash flow is a direct result of lack of Revenue and Profit.

Let's start with a more thorough understanding of the Income Statement, or P&L. Here is a good description; Revenue less Expenses equals Profit/Loss. Three distinct categories.

The Income Statement ...

R - E = P

Revenue *(Sales)*
Expenses
Profit *(Income)*

Measures the financial performance of the business over a certain period of time ...

The Income Statement is a result of tracking Revenue and Expenses over a period of time. All financial reports have three pieces. Let's break down the Income statement into its three distinct pieces, Revenue, Expense and Profit/ Loss.

Remember Revenue is generated by the Employee hat in the business. Revenue represents money paid for doing the job, whatever the job is. There is an exchange of goods/services for tangible funds. So how do you track Revenue in your business?

It starts with the Chart of Accounts:

4000 –4999: Revenue accounts

Why so many accounts for Revenue? Simply put, if you choose to manage it you must measure it. Think of your business. How many different things do you provide service for or sell? How many of these do you track separately in order to understand if you are getting the results you need? How many different things do you need to track? You have 999 accounts you can use. How many are you using?

Many companies when they start out lump all of their sales or revenue into one line item and call it creatively Sales. At some point they realize that it may be beneficial to start breaking out different pieces of the business. How do you determine what to track?

Here are some simple questions to help you decide:

Do you have an area of the business focused on it?
Do you have specific pricing for it?
Do you have specific costs associated with it?
Do you have separate marketing devoted to it?
Are there fixed assets used in the generation of it?

If the answer to any of these questions is yes, then that revenue area needs its own line item. You will need to open up an account and start tracking the revenue through that account. It is important to understand that consistency in measurement will bring better results. So when you are ready, open up the revenue accounts and start using them consistently.

Let's use Charlie's business as an example. Charlie does service and repair work for retail and commercial customers. Charlie also has a couple of tow trucks and sells used cars he has bought and repaired. With these different types of revenue generating pieces of the business, Charlie would like to know which one is most profitable and which one is least profitable. Therefore Charlie needs to track the revenue and cost for each of these parts of the business separately so he can find the answer to his profitability question.

Charlie's revenue accounts would look something like this:

4100 Commercial Repairs
4200 Retail Repairs
4300 Commercial Service
4400 Retail Service
4500 Commercial Towing
4600 Retail Towing
4700 Car Sales

By tracking all of these parts of the business Charlie can see where the revenue is coming from and also use the information in planning and budgeting.

The next part of the Income Statement to discuss is expenses. Expenses are broken into two main parts, variable expenses and fixed expenses. Expenses or costs are tracked to help the business owner determine if you are making money or profit. This is the Manager hat in the business as it relates to money. It is the manager's role to determine if a profit is being made from revenue after covering all expenses.

Here is a reminder of the terminology we discussed in Part 2:

Glossary of Financial Terms

1. Income Statement / Profit Loss Statement
   a) List the revenues and expenses
   b) Shows the results of operations for a period of time: monthly, quarterly and annually

2. Fixed Costs
    a) Costs that do not change in total as business activity increases or decreases. Examples include rent, property insurance and property taxes
3. Variable Costs
    a) Costs that increase in total proportionately with an increase in activy decreases proportionately with a decrease in activity. Examples include direct materials, direct labor and utilities

Let's start with variable expenses or costs first. These are costs in the business that will change proportionately with revenue. So as revenue increases your variable costs will increase. As revenue decreases, your variable costs will decrease. As a business owner that is growing their business and revenue you want your variable cost to increase. I will say that again. When you grow your business you want to see your costs increase. What you also would like to see is these costs, as a percentage of revenue, decrease. Total costs up, as a percentage of revenue down.

Here are the accounts we have from our chart of accounts to manage our variable costs:

5000–5999: cost of goods sold or cost of sales

Previously we discussed some questions around understanding what to track on the revenue side. These same questions pertain to the tracking of your variable costs. If you have created a line item for revenue, then you will want to track the corresponding variable costs for that item.

Do you have an area of the business focused on it?
Do you have specific pricing for it?
Do you have specific costs associated with it?
Do you have separate marketing devoted to it?
Are there fixed assets used in the generation of it?

If the answer to any of these questions is yes, then we must track these variable costs separately. Examples of variable costs would be; Direct Labor, Sub-Contractors, Equipment, Materials and Supplies. These expenses or costs will increase and decrease as the amount of revenue generated increases and decreases. We will discuss the implications of this tracking later in this section when we go over the idea of break even.

Let's continue to use Charlie's business as an example. As we mentioned, Charlie does service and repair work for retail and commercial customers. Charlie also has a couple of tow trucks and sells used cars he has bought and repaired. With these different types of business, Charlie would like to know the profitability of each. Therefore Charlie also needs to track the variable cost for each of these parts of the business so he can find the answer to his profitability question.

Charlie's Cost of Goods Sold accounts would look something like this:

5100 Commercial Repair Costs — Parts
5110 Commercial Repair Costs — Labor
5200 Retail Repair Costs — Parts
5210 Retail Repair Costs — Labor
5300 Commercial Service Costs — Parts
5310 Commercial Service Costs — Labor
5400 Retail Service Costs — Parts
5410 Retail Service Costs — Labor
5500 Commercial Towing Costs
5600 Retail Towing Costs
5700 Car Sale Costs

Within each of these categories there may be many more line items which would roll up into these line items. By tracking all of these expenses of the business Charlie can see where the resources of the company are being used. He can also use the information in planning and budgeting.

These variable expenses, as we stated, are grouped into the category of Cost of Goods sold or Cost of Sales. These expenses represent the direct cost of revenue generation. Therefore what we would like to know as business owners is just how much of every revenue dollar do we get to keep after paying for these direct costs. This is known as Gross Profit.

Revenue - Variable Expenses = Gross Profit

Gross Profit is the result of producing revenue. As we mentioned before, this is the Manager role in the business as it relates to Money. There are two main fundamental pieces of managing Gross Profit, Pricing and Job Cost Control. Pricing decisions are made to make sure the business is maximizing the gross profit on each job or widget at the sale and job costing is maximizing the gross profit on each job or widget during production.

Gross Profit is usually tracked as a percentage of Revenue in the business, known as Gross Profit Margin.

Gross Profit/Revenue = Gross Profit Margin %

or

(Revenue - Variable Exp) ÷ Revenue = Gross Profit Margin %

Gross Profit Margin % (GPM %) is one of the most important pieces of information in business. This percentage is a direct result of your pricing and productivity. It is one of the most critical KPI's (Key Performance Indicators) in your business. We will be using Gross Profit Margin % (GPM %) when we discuss the Break Even Formula later in this section.

The remaining type of cost in your business would be fixed costs. A fixed cost is a cost that does not change in proportion to revenue. Another way to think about it would be if you closed your doors to your customers and remained in business, which expenses would you still have to pay for?

Here are the accounts we have from our chart of accounts to manage our fixed costs:

6000–6999: expense accounts or fixed costs

One of the ways that you can think about fixed costs is that they create capacity. Rents, admin labor and business insurance are great examples of this idea in action. Another type of fixed cost is strictly stuff that you need to stay in business. Office supplies, cleaning and building maintenance are great examples of these types of costs. That is why fixed costs are sometimes referred to as overhead.

Let's look at Charlie's fixed expenses as an example. Charlie would like to know how much money it takes to open the doors of his shop every month. Therefore Charlie needs to track the fixed expenses of his business or the expenses he would have to pay regardless of whether he repaired anything or not.

Charlie's fixed expense accounts would look something like this:

6100 Rent
6200 Wages — Office
6300 Payroll Taxes — Office
6400 Business Insurance
6500 Office Supplies
6600 Advertising and Marketing
6700 Utilities

By tracking all of these fixed expenses Charlie can see where he is investing in his business and also use the information in planning and budgeting.

The goal is to minimize your fixed costs while growing your capacity to produce revenue. This, when combined with maximizing your gross profit margin percentage, will maximize your net profit.

Revenue - Variable Expenses = Gross Profit

Gross Profit - Fixed Expenses = Net Profit

Increasing Revenue will increase your variable expenses and your gross profit. Increasing your gross profit while keeping steady or lowering your fixed costs will increase your net profit. Revenue goes up, total expenses go up and profit goes up. This is what a growing business looks like.

So now we have discussed the three sections of an Income Statement or P & L. Revenue, Expenses and Profit. Revenue is generated through the Employee Hat, Expenses and Profit is managed by the Manager Hat. So now let's move on to the concept of Break Even.

Calculating break-even ...

BE = FC ÷ GP%

BE = *Revenue required to Break-Even*
FC = *Fixed Costs*
GP% = *Gross Profit margin*

Gross Profit margin % = Gross Profit ÷ Revenue

Gross Profit = Revenue - variable costs

Break Even in your business represents the amount of revenue you need to produce at your current gross profit margin % to cover your fixed costs. It is called break even because there is no profit and there is no loss. It is just enough to keep going. There are usually not too many business owners that get into business with the goal of break even, yet many are there today. The best reason to know this formula is that it will help you get above your break even and stay there.

So let's take a look at the formula. Your break even revenue is equal to your total fixed costs divided by your gross profit margin %. Why is this true? Let's think about it. Using some very simple numbers, we can see how the formula makes sense.

We will again use Charlie's garage as an example to help you understand the concept. Say Charlie has a 50% GPM. That means that for every dollar of revenue Charlie receives, he gets to keep 50 cents. Let's also say that he has $1,000 of fixed costs a month. Therefore Charlie's BE = FC / GPM% or $2,000 = $1,000/50%. His break even amount in sales or revenue is $2,000 according to the formula. Let's put a simple P&L together for his business. Remember, revenue less expenses equals profit.

$2,000 – ($2,000 x 50% + $1,000) = 0

OR

Revenue	$2,000	
Variable Exp	$1,000	*((1–50%) of Revenue)*
Gross Profit	$1,000	
Fixed Exp	$1,000	
Net Profit	0	

Charlie produced $2,000 in revenue, had a Gross Profit of $1,000 and had fixed expenses of $1,000 for the month. Let's change some of the numbers and see what happens to his business. What would happen if Charlie increased his fixed costs to $2,000 a month?

BE = FC ÷ GPM% or $4,000 = $2,000 ÷ 50%,

$4,000 - ($4,000 x 50% + $2,000) = 0

OR

Revenue	$4,000	
Variable Exp	$2,000	*((1–50%) of Revenue)*
Gross Profit	$2,000	
Fixed Exp	$2,000	
Net Profit	0	

Charlie now needs to produce $4,000 a month to get to the same place. His business is now twice as big yet produces the same profitability.

Let's go back to the original numbers. Let's say Charlie only has a 25% GPM instead of 50%. What is his new break even?

BE = FC ÷ GPM% or **$4,000 = $1,000 ÷ 25%,**

$4,000 - ($4,000 x **75% + $1,000) = 0**

OR

Revenue	$4,000	
Variable Exp	$3,000	*((1–25%) of Revenue)*
Gross Profit	$1,000	
Fixed Exp	$1,000	
Net Profit	0	

The business still needs to be twice as big to produce the same results. Think about the formula again. If your fixed costs go up, your break even in revenue goes up. If you're Gross Profit Margin % goes down, your break even goes up. You have probably already noticed these things happening in your business. When your suppliers raise their prices and you do not keep pace, your break even goes up. When you need bigger space or another person, your break even goes up.

What about the opposite? What if you raise your prices? What happens to your GPM%? If you raise your prices, your revenue goes up while your variable costs stay the same so your GPM% goes up. Therefore your break even goes down. We will discuss more about pricing later in this part.

So let's walk through an example of how to calculate this in your business. Remember you need to know your fixed expenses and your Gross Profit Margin % in order to calculate your break even.

On the following page is a step-by-step process to help you understand how to calculate break even in your business.

Break-Even Calculator — Example

1. **Total Monthly Expenses**	**$ 20,000.00**
2. **Total Monthly Fixed Expenses**	**5,000.00**
3. **Total Monthly Variable Expenses** *(1 less 2)*	
4. **Total Monthly Revenue**	**25,000.00**
5. **Monthly Gross Profit** *(4 less 3)*	
6. **Gross Profit Margin %** *(5 divided by 4)*	
7. **Monthly Breakeven Revenue** *(2 divided by 6)*	

Instructions:

a. Enter Total Monthly Expenses on Line 1
b. Enter Monthly Fixed Expenses on Line 2
c. Subtract Line 2 from Line 1 to calculate Total Monthly Variable Expenses *(Line 3)*
d. Enter Total Monthly Revenue on Line 4
e. Subtract Line 3 from Line 4 to calculate Monthly Gross Profit *(Line 5)*
f. Divide Line 5 by Line 4 to calculate Gross Profit Margin % *(Line 6)*
g. Divide Line 2 by Line 6 to calculate Monthly Break-even Revenue *(Line 7)*

In this example the business has monthly revenue of $25,000 (Line 4) and has monthly expenses of $20,000 (Line 1). The P&L of this business would look like this:

Revenue ($25,000) – Expenses ($20,000) = Profit ($5,000)

This business had a net profit of $5,000 for the month. Great! We have a net profit. That's fantastic! What we want to know is based on this companies breakout between fixed and variable costs, what is the monthly amount of revenue this business needs to achieve to cover their fixed costs and therefore achieve a profit on a consistent basis.

Let's start by using the example. As you can see, this business owner knows they have $20,000 in total costs for the month (Step A). They have also taken out their P&L and walked through all of the expenses and determined by the previous definitions which of these costs are fixed. They pulled out rent, the admin salary, insurance and office supplies and that number came to $5,000 for the month (Step B). We now have the first piece of the puzzle, fixed costs, answered. So now they can calculate the next line (Step C).

Break-Even Calculator — Example

1. **Total Monthly Expenses**	**$ 20,000.00**
2. **Total Monthly Fixed Expenses**	**5,000.00**
3. **Total Monthly Variable Expenses** *(1 less 2)*	**15,000.00**
4. **Total Monthly Revenue**	**25,000.00**
5. **Monthly Gross Profit** *(4 less 3)*	
6. **Gross Profit Margin %** *(5 divided by 4)*	
7. **Monthly Breakeven Revenue** *(2 divided by 6)*	

Instructions:

a. Enter Total Monthly Expenses on Line 1
b. Enter Monthly Fixed Expenses on Line 2
c. Subtract Line 2 from Line 1 to calculate Total Monthly Variable Expenses *(Line 3)*
d. Enter Total Monthly Revenue on Line 4
e. Subtract Line 3 from Line 4 to calculate Monthly Gross Profit *(Line 5)*
f. Divide Line 5 by Line 4 to calculate Gross Profit Margin % *(Line 6)*
g. Divide Line 2 by Line 6 to calculate Monthly Break-even Revenue *(Line 7)*

You now know for the month they had $15,000 in variable expenses. Why is this important? Well in order to determine your GPM%, you need to know your revenue and your variable costs. The revenue for the month is $25,000 (Step D). Now we can finish the formula by following Step E.

Break-Even Calculator — Example

1. **Total Monthly Expenses**	**$ 20,000.00**
2. **Total Monthly Fixed Expenses**	**5,000.00**
3. **Total Monthly Variable Expenses** *(1 less 2)*	**15,000.00**
4. **Total Monthly Revenue**	**25,000.00**
5. **Monthly Gross Profit** *(4 less 3)*	**10,000.00**
6. **Gross Profit Margin %** *(5 divided by 4)*	**40%**
7. **Monthly Breakeven Revenue** *(2 divided by 6)*	**12,500.00**

Instructions:

a. Enter Total Monthly Expenses on Line 1
b. Enter Monthly Fixed Expenses on Line 2
c. Subtract Line 2 from Line 1 to calculate Total Monthly Variable Expenses *(Line 3)*
d. Enter Total Monthly Revenue on Line 4
e. Subtract Line 3 from Line 4 to calculate Monthly Gross Profit *(Line 5)*
f. Divide Line 5 by Line 4 to calculate Gross Profit Margin % *(Line 6)*
g. Divide Line 2 by Line 6 to calculate Monthly Break-even Revenue *(Line 7)*

This business has $10,000 in gross profit as shown in Line 5. Completing Step F produces our GPM% of 40% as shown above. We now have the second piece of the puzzle and are ready to calculate our monthly break even amount. Reviewing the Formula (BE = FC / GPM %) allows us to complete the example as shown in Step G above.

Our monthly break even in revenue is $12,500. We need to produce $12,500 in revenue at a gross profit margin of 40% to cover our $5,000 in fixed costs a month. Let's do the math backward to confirm.

Rev ($12,500) * GPM (40%) = Fixed Costs ($5,000)

So how much revenue did this company do in the month? $25,000. If we only needed to get to $12,500 to break even, what did the amount above this number produce for the business?

Rev ($25,000 - $12,500 = $12,500) * GPM (40%) =???

How much profit did this business make for the month? $5,000? What is $12,500 times 40%? $5,000! The first $12,500 of revenue was needed to cover fixed costs; the extra $12,500 in revenue was needed to produce a profit.

A quick test of the validity of the formula is to recalculate your break even by adding profit to your fixed costs. Let's give it a try with our example.

Revenue = (FC ($5,000) + Profit ($5,000))/ GPM (40%)

Revenue = $10,000/ 40% = $25,000

We have now backed into our monthly revenue of $25,000 by adding our profit to our fixed cost. Here is an interesting thought. What if you treated profit like a fixed expense? Would you always pay it? Most business owners pay their rent or mortgage, payroll and other expenses every month because they know they need to in order to stay in business. How many times have you missed paying profit? What if you paid your profit out on the first business day of the month like rent? Would you be able to make it back by the end of the month?

What if this business owner concentrated on just breaking even? They would only produce $12,500 of revenue a month because that is all they need. Would they plan to make only $12,500 and hope to bring in more? What are your plans around profit? Do you consistently create it?

Now it is time to calculate your own break even revenue. You can use the template on the following page to work through your own numbers.

First, let's discuss what you will need to get started. You will need your latest Income Statement or P&L (Accrual Based). Depending on how long you have been in business, it is best to use the average of the last six to twelve months as a starting point. If you have just started in business, you are going to have to estimate along the way.

We need to start with your total expenses. Add up all of your average monthly expenses and drop that number into Line 1. Then, as we described previously in this section, go back through each of your expense accounts and decide if they are fixed or variable. Once again, start with the fixed and ask yourself if you would still have to pay for it if you do not produce any revenue. Make your best judgment call. If you are wrong, you will find out when you are monitoring your P&L monthly.

When you have decided what your average monthly fixed expenses are, drop them into Line 2. Compute Line 3. Take the average monthly revenue and fill in Line 4 then proceed to calculate Line 5, 6 and Line 7. What is your answer? How do you know if it makes any sense?

Here is quick test. Add your average monthly profit for the time period you are looking at to your fixed costs. Recalculate your break even in revenue. It should equal the amount you placed on the worksheet.

Break-Even Calculator — Yours

1. **Total Monthly Expenses**	
2. **Total Fixed Expenses**	
3. **Total Monthly Variable Expenses** *(1 less 2)*	
4. **Total Monthly Revenue**	
5. **Monthly Gross Profit** *(4 less 3)*	
6. **Gross Profit Margin %** *(5 divided by 4)*	
7. **Monthly Breakeven Revenue** *(2 divided by 6)*	

Instructions:

a. Enter Total Monthly Expenses on Line 1
b. Enter Monthly Fixed Expenses on Line 2
c. Subtract Line 2 from Line 1 to calculate Total Monthly Variable Expenses *(Line 3)*
d. Enter Total Monthly Revenue on Line 4
e. Subtract Line 3 from Line 4 to calculate Monthly Gross Profit *(Line 5)*
f. Divide Line 5 by Line 4 to calculate Gross Profit Margin % *(Line 6)*
g. Divide Line 2 by Line 6 to calculate Monthly Break-even Revenue *(Line 7)*

Are you surprised by your results? Do they make sense? Are they consistent with your pricing? Did you realize how much in expenses you are starting with in the month before you even produce revenue?

If you are unsure of your results, redo the worksheet with different periods. If you have recently made significant changes to the business, it is always a good idea to go back and recalculate your number.

There are many different types of businesses and all of them have a potential to produce profits. Some businesses are high margin-high fixed cost businesses like a professional services company. Some are the opposite, low margin-low overhead or fixed cost businesses like online retailers. You can also have a low margin-high fixed cost business like construction.

There are many ways to find out the normal gross profit margin percent for your industry. Ask your accountant to help you find out and then compare it to yours. If you are higher, how do you keep it that way? If you are lower, what do you need to do to get it back closer to the average?

Let's take a look at your pricing. How do you determine what your goods or services will sell for in your market? Most business owners have let the market determine their pricing. Most have worried about the lowest cost providers in their market and have priced to them in order to win or keep the business. This creates a business where everyone is busy, but there never seems to be enough money to create a decent profit. Customers are unhappy with the results because there is tremendous pressure to win the new job and get it done. Business becomes busyness and everyone is unhappy.

What would happen if you started with the quality of work you do and willingness of the market to pay for that quality? If you believe customers only care about price, you will attract price shoppers to your business. If you believe there are customers that will pay for quality, then what would your pricing look like?

Here is some simple math when it comes to raising or lowering your prices. Take a look at the chart below. Find you current GPM% and take a look at what raising your prices would do to your business.

If Your Present Margin Is ...

And You *Increase* Your Price by ...

Your sales would have to DECLINE by the amount shown before your Profit is reduced ...

	20%	**25%**	**30%**	**35%**	**40%**	**45%**	**50%**	**55%**	**60%**
2%	9%	7%	6%	5%	5%	4%	4%	4%	3%
4%	17%	14%	12%	10%	9%	8%	7%	7%	6%
6%	23%	19%	17%	15%	13%	12%	11%	10%	9%
8%	29%	24%	21%	19%	17%	15%	14%	13%	12%
10%	33%	29%	25%	22%	20%	18%	17%	15%	14%
12%	38%	32%	29%	26%	23%	21%	19%	18%	17%

	20%	25%	30%	35%	40%	45%	50%	55%	60%
14%	41%	36%	32%	29%	26%	24%	22%	20%	19%
16%	44%	39%	35%	31%	29%	26%	24%	23%	21%
18%	47%	42%	38%	34%	31%	29%	26%	25%	23%
20%	50%	44%	40%	36%	33%	31%	29%	27%	25%
25%	56%	50%	45%	42%	38%	36%	33%	31%	29%
30%	60%	55%	50%	46%	43%	40%	38%	35%	33%

So if your present GPM% is 20% and you raised your prices by 10% you could lose 33% of your business and make the same amount of money. Imagine doing a third less business and making the same amount of money. What would that be like? Even if your margin is twice as large, 40%, you could still lose a fifth of your clients or customers and still make the same exact amount of profit. What fears do you have around raising prices? Is losing customers one of them? Does this help change your mind around those fears?

If you are currently discounting to get customers, take a look at the next chart shown below.

If Your Present Margin is ...

And You *Discount* Your Price by ...

Your sales must INCREASE by the amount shown below to keep the ***same*** *margin ...*

	20%	25%	30%	35%	40%	45%	50%	55%	60%
2%	11%	9%	7%	6%	5%	5%	4%	4%	3%
4%	25%	19%	15%	13%	11%	10%	9%	8%	7%
6%	43%	32%	25%	21%	18%	15%	14%	12%	11%
8%	67%	47%	36%	30%	25%	22%	19%	17%	15%
10%	100%	67%	50%	40%	33%	29%	25%	22%	20%
12%	150%	92%	67%	52%	43%	36%	32%	28%	25%
14%	233%	127%	88%	67%	54%	45%	39%	34%	30%
16%	400%	178%	114%	84%	67%	55%	47%	41%	36%
18%	900%	257%	150%	106%	82%	67%	56%	49%	43%

	20%	25%	30%	35%	40%	45%	50%	55%	60%
20%	-	400%	200%	133%	100%	80%	67%	57%	50%
25%	-	-	500%	250%	167%	125%	100%	83%	71%
30%	-	-	-	600%	300%	200%	150%	120%	100%

If your GPM% is 20% you would have to double your business to make the same profit. If doing twice as much work nets the same results, why would you do it? If you are discounting, stop it!

There are also many ways to find out the normal fixed costs as a percentage of revenue for your industry. Ask your accountant to help you find out and then compare it to yours. If you are lower, how do you keep it that way? If you are higher, what do you need to do to get it back closer to the average?

Fixed costs are in essence the capacity that you have built. The real question you have to ask yourself is what amount of your capacity are you using on a monthly basis? If it is not enough, then you can either reduce capacity or increase revenue. It is your choice, but you have to do something or you will continue to put cash flow pressure on your business with an overcapacity issue.

So back to your break even analysis. There are really multiple ways to look at break even. The amount of revenue you need to produce to cover your fixed costs is what could be called initial break even or Break Even 1 (BE1). Break Even 1 (BE1) is a great goal for a new or start up business. It takes time to grow a customer base and if you do not have one there are investments that you need to make to create a business.

Break Even 2 (BE2) is where you have reached BE1 and you are also covering your debt payment. Repayment of debt is not part of your income statement, yet needs to come out of your operating cash flow in order to stay in business. There are many business owners who are constantly flirting with BE2 and actually adding to debt over time instead of paying it off. Many business owners have used a line of credit to cover operating cash flow deficiencies with an idea of paying it back someday, but never really creating a plan to make it happen.

Break Even 3 (BE3) is where the business is consistently at BE2 and now starts to produce a return for the owner. How much profit do you need to make?

We examined this idea when we walked through the Dreams x Goals x Plan x Activity section. Many business owners find it hard to plan for their dreams when they are scratching to make Break Even 1. Step one is creating consistency. Without consistency, the business will continue to drop below BE1 and add to the debt making getting to BE2 even more difficult.

Let's use Charlie's business as an example. Charlie has been moving from below Break Even 1 to above Break Even 3 the entire time he has owned the business. He has used his line of credit to keep the business going in the lean times and has attempted to pay down the line when possible. He has sporadically paid himself and will forgo a paycheck when necessary to keep from borrowing more from the line of credit.

As we have seen, Charlie has a Gross Profit Margin of 50%. He also has fixed expenses of $10,000 a month including his wage for the work he does in the business. He has an outstanding balance of $24,000 on his line of credit that he would like to pay off in two years and he would like to have a consistent $5,000 profit every month. Here are his Break Even calculations:

BE1 = $10,000 / 50% = $20,000
BE2 = ($10,000 + $1,000) / 50% = $22,000
BE3 = ($10,000 + $1,000 + $5,000) / 50% = $34,000

Charlie needs to consistently produce $34,000 of revenue at a 50% margin monthly to achieve his dreams. What are your Break Even numbers?

BE1 = $________ / ____% = $________
BE2 = ($________ + $________) / ____% = $________
BE3 = ($________ + $________ + $________) / ____% = $________

What other business decisions can you make with the break even formula? Have you ever had to decide if you were going to change your margin or add some capacity to your business? How could you use the formula to help you determine the impact on your business before you act?

We have already discussed raising or lowering your prices. What about the decision to initiate a sales training program? The first thing we need to know is the investment in the training. Let's say Charlie was willing to invest $10,000 in training. His current margin is 50% so he would need an additional $20,000 in sales to make the training pay for itself. (BE = FC/GPM% or $20,000 = $10,000/50%).

What if Charlie was finally ready to hire that administrative person to do all those things that he hates to do so he can actually spend time growing the business? Let's say that the admin person would cost $3,000 a month. Using Charlie's current margin of 50% we would calculate that he would need an additional $6,000 in sales to be able to cover the cost of the admin person. (BE = FC/GPM% or $6,000 = $3,000/50%).

Take a moment and list five things that you know you need to invest in the business to grow and calculate how much more in revenue you need to achieve to make them pay for themselves.

1.) .... Rev .... =FC .... /GPM% ....
2.) .... Rev .... =FC .... /GPM% ....
3.) .... Rev .... =FC .... /GPM% ....
4.) .... Rev .... =FC .... /GPM% ....
5.) .... Rev .... =FC .... /GPM% ....

What did you learn? Are there some things that you can invest in immediately that will provide you an excellent return? Are there some things that won't work after all? Are you comfortable enough with the formula to use it to make these types of business decisions?

The point is, if you know what return you need to get from an investment, the higher the probability that investment will pay off. Understanding your Gross Profit Margin percentage and tracking your Fixed Costs or Expenses will allow you to make rational business choices based on a projected rate of return instead of just a hope that it will work.

It may take you some time to get proficient at calculating your break even. Calculate it enough times so that it becomes second nature to you and your team. Ask the right questions, use your best assumptions and track the results. You will get better each and every month. It just takes practice and time. We will be building on this information as we continue. If you think you need to invest more time on this part before we move on, redo the worksheets and gain some confidence.

We have now covered the Income Statement or P&L and calculating your Break Even. We are now ready to move on to the Balance Sheet and business valuation. Now are you ready to discuss building equity?

Review

Do you remember the Rule of Three's when it comes to the Income Statement?

The Income Statement ...

R - E = P

Revenue *(Sales)*
Expenses
Profit *(Income)*

Measures the financial performance of the business over a certain period of time ...

Have your properly segregated your costs into fixed and variable components? Do you have your business lines set up to be able to measure the Gross Profit Margin for each one? Did you set up a profit account where you put your money into on the first of every month?

Do you have a plan put together with your accountant to help get you financial statements under control? Have you an agreed upon time schedule to review your statements on a monthly basis? Have you been able to determine your Break Even in Revenue and possibly other Break Even metrics in your business?

Calculating break-even ...

BE = FC ÷ GP%

BE = *Revenue required to Break-Even*

FC = *Fixed Costs*

GP% = *Gross Profit margin*

Gross Profit margin % = Gross Profit ÷ Revenue

Gross Profit = Revenue - variable costs

What will it take for you to be ready to make business investment decisions using the break even formula? What are the areas of your business you need to invest in and what would be the payback period for each investment? When are you going to start taking more measured risk in your business?

PART 4

The Balance Sheet, Equity and Business Valuation

One way to look at the success of the business is to look at the profit generated by the business. This profit is shown on the Income Statement as we discussed in Part 3. Another form of success the business creates is the value of the business itself. All business owners are replaced in their business at some point. What happens to most business owners is they think this day will somehow magically appear and a smooth transition will happen without planning.

Succession planning is something most business owners understand must happen yet very few take action. What does the Balance Sheet have to do with succession planning? Simple. The Balance Sheet, as we described earlier, breaks down the business into what you own versus what you owe, and the corresponding equity between the two. Here at ActionCOACH, our definition of a business is "A commercial, profitable, saleable enterprise that works without you". The key here is to create a predictable stream of cash flows for which people will gladly pay you.

Employees create money for their retirement by saving a percentage of their annual salary each year until they have accumulated enough to live on the rest of their life. Business owners can use a different model. By creating a stream of predictable cash flows that someone else would be willing to buy, the reinvestment of annual cash flows can usually create a larger return for the business owner than stocks or bonds or mutual funds. This is the main difference between having a job and owning a company. Return on investment!

Let's start by looking at the Balance Sheet. The Chart of Accounts uses these sections for the Balance Sheet:

1000–1999: asset accounts
2000–2999: liability accounts
3000–3999: equity accounts

Glossary of Financial Terms

1. Balance Sheet
   - **a)** Shows the financial position of a company at a particular point in time
   - **b)** Allows the reader to view the total resources of the company and determine how the assets are being financed
   - **c)** Is a record of the liquidity of the business and the owner's equity at a given point in time
   - **d)** It's a snapshot of the business that shows what the business owns and what the business owes
2. Assets
   - **a)** What is owned by the company: cash, accounts receivable, inventories and plant and equipment: recorded at acquisition price
3. Liabilities
   - **a)** What the company owes: accounts payable, loans, credit card balances and unpaid sales and payroll taxes
4. Owner Equity
   - **a)** Difference between what you have and what you owe

Let's start with a more thorough understanding of the Balance Sheet. Here is a good description; Assets less Liabilities equals Equity. Once again, three distinct categories ...

The Balance Sheet ...

A - L = OE

Assets
Liabilities
Owner Equity

Measures the financial condition of the business at a certain point in time ...

As we discussed earlier, assets are what you own. Let's break this down into the different types of assets, Current and Fixed. Current Assets are assets which are either cash or something that can be turned into cash in a short period of time, usually less than 90 days. Examples of Current Assets are Cash, Accounts Receivable, Inventory, Prepaid Expenses, and anything else you own which can be turned into cash.

Current Assets or liquid assets are important to monitor because they represent the lifeblood of the business. Cash management is one of the most important things a business must do in order to grow. The Balance Sheet, specifically current assets, helps the business owner monitor cash and cash equivalents. We will discuss cash management in much more detail in Part 5.

Fixed Assets are things like land, equipment, vehicles, and anything else you own that most likely you will keep for a while and are not thinking of turning into cash. Fixed Assets also can gain or lose value over time. Land, for example can increase in value over time. Vehicles slowly lose their value over time as they are used to create revenue in the business.

Fixed assets are also very important to monitor as they represent an investment in the business. It is important to make sure your Balance Sheet properly reflects these investments. Most companies keep a list of fixed assets that can be modified as the business buys and sells equipment and vehicles over the year. The Fixed Asset section of the Balance Sheet should include all other the stuff the business owns as to create a true picture of the overall worth of the business.

The Fixed Asset section of the Balance Sheet will also include depreciation. Depreciation by definition is a noncash expense that reduces the value of an asset as a result of wear, tear, age, or obsolescence. You can think about depreciation as a way to capture the loss of value through use of your fixed assets. It is also important to note that depreciation is a noncash expense and therefore reduces your bottom line but there is no monthly cash outlay. This is due to the fact that you either 1.) Paid cash for the asset initially or 2.) Are making monthly payments on the asset and that is the cash part of the transaction.

A good example of how to explain depreciation would be look at a piece of equipment. Let's say you need a new piece of equipment that costs $12,000. The average life of this piece of equipment is 5 years. Your accountant tells you that according to the rules you must depreciate this asset over the five year period using the straight line method. Therefore, you will lower the value of the asset and create an expense of $200 a month for five years. $12,000 divided by 60 months equals $200 a month.

The $200 of depreciation expense stops after five years, but the cost to maintain the asset has been climbing over the last couple of years as equipment tends to break down more often as it ages. Many business owners struggle to understand when to replace old fixed assets. Looking at the maintenance on the old piece of equipment plus the opportunity cost of having the equipment out of service versus the cost of new equipment is a good way to analyze the situation.

The asset would be on your Balance sheet at $12,000 the first month and by the end of the five years would be at zero. Now that piece of equipment may have some residual value left after five years, but the balance sheet will not reflect that value. If you sell the equipment at that point there would be a gain on the sale which has other tax implications but would simply disappear from the Balance Sheet.

Looking at your annual monthly maintenance costs plus the lost revenue from the downtime minus that annual cost of a new piece of equipment should allow you to make a decision when the asset is fully depreciated. Most business owners try to squeeze the last ounce of life out of their assets. That makes sense. Just make sure you are taking into consideration all of your costs and downtime.

Buildings and land are dealt with differently. They are placed on the Balance Sheet at what is called Historical Cost and left there at that value until they are disposed of. Here is actual rule used to determine how to value a non-depreciable asset; (1) the cost principle directs the accountant to report the company's assets at their original historical cost, and (2) the monetary unit assumption directs the accountant to presume the U.S. dollar is stable over time—it is not affected by inflation or deflation.

Many of the company's most valuable assets are not even on the Balance Sheet due to this rule. People, trademarks, your brand and many other things that other businesses would pay money for are not listed as an asset. This is important to understand when we discuss business valuation later in this section. The Balance Sheet does not reflect what you could sell your business for, but does hold many clues as to what your business is worth.

The last section relating to assets would be Other. Other is a great way accountants have come up with to classify stuff which doesn't fit the before mentioned parts, Current and Fixed. Some typical other assets are deposits for leases, deposits held with other business or anything you own which doesn't fall under the other two classifications.

So to using the rule of three's we can review the Asset side of the Balance Sheet which is broken down into three components, Current, Fixed and Other. Current Assets are cash or cash equivalents. Fixed Assets are long term holdings and Other Assets are anything which doesn't fit the first two. Remember that Assets reflect what the business owns, so if you own it and you can quantify it, it should be on the Balance Sheet. If it is on the Balance Sheet, you own it.

Let's move on to the Liability section of the Balance Sheet, otherwise known as what you owe. Once again there are three main sections to this part; Current, Long Term and Other. Current Liabilities are just the opposite of Current Assets; it is money you owe to other people within a relatively short period of time.

Some examples of Current Liabilities are; Accounts Payable, payroll liabilities, lines of credit and anything else considered short term money which is owed to someone else. This section of the Balance Sheet is used to help the business owner understand how much the business owes to others due to the result of creating revenue.

Accounts Payable is usually attributed to vendors a business would use in the course of revenue creation. Payroll liabilities are also a result of revenue generation, and short term use of the line of credit is due to mismatches in the timing of collections from customers and the payment of bills from vendors and payroll.

There are a couple of important clues the business owner can get from this section of the balance sheet in conjunction with Current Assets. The Current

Ratio is a ratio business owners can use to help understand and predict cash flow over a short period of time. This is also known as Working Capital. Here is the ratio, as defined below:

Current Ratio = Current Assets/Current Liabilities

As we mentioned before, Current Assets are cash or cash equivalents owed to the business over a short period of time. Current Liabilities are cash equivalents owed to others of a short period of time. In a healthy business, this ration will be well over 1:1 and trend toward a higher level as the company becomes more profitable.

Understanding this ratio can help any business owner with cash flow issues pinpoint exactly where the issues are coming from. If your ratio is below 1:1, then some part of your business is keeping cash away when you need it most. Retail businesses which collect cash at the time of transaction and have little to no Accounts Receivable have different issues than a business which is entirely based on receivables and has a large Accounts Payable amount as well.

Businesses that carry inventory versus just-in-time companies will also have different issues when it comes to cash flow. Another ratio which can be used for inventory intensive businesses is the Quick Ratio.

Quick Ratio = (Current Assets – Inventory**)** ÷ Current Liabilities

This ratio removes inventory from the equation so the business owner has a good idea of what is happening with Cash Flow when inventory turns. So you can see how important it is to make sure you have classified all of your liabilities correctly so you can use these ratios to predict your upcoming cash flow. We will discuss cash flow forecasting in great detail in Part 5.

The next part of the liability section of the Balance Sheet is Long Term Liabilities. Examples of these types of things that as a business owner you owe would be loans, long term leases and notes payable. Sometimes your accountant will take the current portion of these borrowings and place them into the Current Liability section of the Balance Sheet per GAAP reporting. This reclassification will help you understand the cash needs of your business on a short term basis with these amounts now included in your Current and Quick Ratios.

The Long term liability section of the balance sheet represents investment made in the long term Asset section. Most business owners understand the importance of using financial leverage in their business. As we discussed in Part 1, Financial Leverage is when you use other people's money (OPM) to invest in the infrastructure of your business to increase capacity and make more money.

OPM or Financial Leverage requires the business owner to calculate their expected return on the investment and have a plan of how to pay back the loan. Banks are in business to lend money. Banks cannot make money without lending it to someone. Banks also operate on razor thin margins so in turn are very anxious to know that they will get their money back. Therefore, banks love to lend businesses money to buy equipment and other fixed assets because they can use those assets as collateral when making a loan.

Take a look at your current Balance Sheet. Have you bought any equipment or vehicles? Did you take out a loan to buy any of those long term assets? You should be able to see the long term asset and the corresponding loan on your balance sheet. You will also see you have some accumulated depreciation against the asset and the amount of the loan has been reduced by the payments you have made to date. These balance sheet items will move lower with each and every month as you depreciate the asset and make your monthly payments.

Once again, you need to keep an eye on the total of your investments and the amount you owe against them. You do not want to owe more than the assets are worth and, as we mentioned before, you may be happy when the payments are over although your maintenance expenses are usually climbing at this point.

So a good way to understand when to use OPM is when you are buying stuff. As a business owner you want to keep your cash to use for things other people will view as a risky investment and will likely be hesitant to lend you money for. Both investments should be based on Financial Leverage not debt, which if you remember is using or borrowing money without a plan of how to pay it back. Just because it is your money does not mean you don't have to pay yourself back!

Having a fixed asset and long term liability plan will go a long way in helping you, the business owner, understand when and how to manage this section of your balance sheet. You want to make sure you are getting a great return on your assets and are using them to the fullest extent possible.

We will discuss these concepts in more detail in the next section. The Balance Sheet has many clues to your upcoming cash flow and it is important to know what to look for and how to use it. At this point stop reading and take out the most recent Balance Sheet for you company and calculate the Ratios we described above. Write your answers in the space below ...

Current Assets ....

Current Ratio .... = -:-

Current Liabilities ....

(Current Assets – Inventory**)** ....

Quick Ratio .... = -:-

Current Liabilities ....

Are you happy with your results? Is your ration well over 1:1? If not, do you know the reason why and do you know how to fix it? If not we will explore these concepts in greater detail in the next section that dives deep into cash flow forecasting.

The last section of the liability portion of the balance sheet is Other. Just like on the asset side, anything that doesn't fall into one of the other two categories is considered Other.

The last section of the Balance Sheet is the Equity section. The equity section of the Balance Sheet represents the investment you, the business owner, made in the business. This section will have line items like Common Stock, Paid in Capital, Retained Earnings and Income. The Income line will represent the amount of income from operations for the current fiscal year. Once you close out a fiscal year that income will become retained earnings.

As we mentioned earlier in this book, it is called a Balance Sheet because by accounting rules it must balance. Assets less Liabilities must equal Equity. Or Assets equals Liabilities plus Equity. In the end things must equal. If you are looking at your Balance Sheet and it does not balance, please see your accountant immediately.

There are a couple of things to understand about the Equity section as a business owner. First, it does give you an idea if your company is growing or not. If the size of the Balance Sheet is growing and your equity position is shrinking, then that probably means you are investing in your business. It could also mean trouble for the business. If the size of the Balance sheet is shrinking and the equity position is growing, it means you are maximizing your return on assets.

Think of your Equity position in your business as the difference in what you own and what you owe. All of us would like to own more than we own, so watching the balance of your equity account, just like any other investment, will let you know the path you are on. It gets a little more complex when you own a business because there are many factors that go into the valuation of a business which may or may not be on the Balance Sheet.

So how do you value a business? There are many different ways to value a business. Some are based on the industry you are in, others are based on different methodologies based on current financial information and still others are based on future cash flow of the business and the potential market share the business can achieve.

The bottom line when it comes to business valuation the beauty is in the eye of the beholder. In the end the business is only worth what someone else is willing to pay for it. This is true for any type of asset or investment. Think of the value of a share of stock of a blue chip company. If this stock is part of an exchange were the value is easy to determine, there are most likely many buyers and sellers within a small variance of a posted price.

Now think of a piece of property. If there are many like properties, the value can be determined and there is most likely a robust market for this asset. Though the more unique the property, the harder to value therefore the harder to sell. As you move further and further away from easily defined prices, the market for the asset becomes harder to determine.

Now think of your business. How many different variables would go into the valuation process for your business? Location, number of customers, type of customers, concentration of customers, competition, pricing, brand, employees, business type, and cash flow are just some of the variables that come to mind. In the end, an investor is looking to buy a predictable stream of cash flows at a discount, based on the risk of those cash flows continuing for a predictable period of time.

Does your business produce a predictable stream of cash flows? How much of the business is based on what you do and who you are? What would happen to the business if something happened to you? One of the hard truths about owning a business is we all exit our business at some point, voluntarily or involuntarily. Let's take another look at our definition of a business, "a commercial, profitable, saleable enterprise that works without you", or otherwise known as a predictable stream of cash flows. If the owner is the main reason the cash flow exists, then the business is not worth much without the owner. This is why you see so many small businesses sell and the owner must stick around for the transition.

What would someone pay for a predictable stream of cash flows? It depends on what valuation model you are using. Sometimes businesses are not worth anything. Sometimes they are worth more due to the value of the idea. So a typical valuation model starts with determining how much true cash flow the business is or can create. This is commonly referred to as EBITDA or Earnings Before Interest, Taxes, Depreciation and Amortization.

The main reason for looking at the cash flow of a business before counting the previously mentioned items is these items will most like change with the ownership of the business. Interest is based on the current debt load of the company. Tax rates are determined by business structure and Depreciation and Amortization on based on the Balance Sheet items the company owns, which will most likely change with the sale.

Another factor the valuation process usually removes when we discuss owner/operator type businesses is the salary and benefits due to ownership. Removing the wage of the owner and any other expenses the owner runs through the business gives a truer picture of cash flow after sale. This is the cash flow someone else will pay for.

Once you have determined the correct amount of cash flow to value the company, you must now come up with what is referred to as a multiple. The multiple is what the cash flow will be multiplied by to calculate the value of the business. This multiple is based on several factors including business type, recurring revenue, systems, customer concentration, potential employee turnover and a host of other possible factors.

This multiple can range from 1 to as high as 10 based on the previously mentioned factors. Generally the more systematized the business, the higher the value. The more recurring revenue that exists the higher the value of the business.

The more contractually based the revenue, the higher the value. The more the employees are bound to the business contractually, the higher the value.

The more time you spend working on the business and making it work without you, the more valuable the business is to someone else. Working on the business is essential to increase your profit, yet the real payoff is when you sell your business for a higher multiple because of your efforts.

Let's look at some examples ...

Business A

Revenue	$1,000,000
Net Profit	100,000
Interest Expense	5,000
Depreciation	20,000
Owner's Salary & Exp	125,000

Let's do the math. First we need to determine the EBITDA or Earnings before Interest, Taxes, Depreciation and Amortization ...

EBITDA =

Earnings *(100,000)* + **I**nterest *(5,000)* +
Depreciation *(20,000)* + **A**mortization (0) = **$125,000**

So our EBITDA is $125,000. We also need to add back the owner's salary and expenses of $125,000 which equals $250,000. Now we need to subtract what it would cost to get someone to take the owner's place, say $75,000. That leaves us at $175,000 ($250,000 – 75,000).

Now we need to determine a multiple for the business. Some of the $1,000,000 in revenue is recurring, but not under contract. Most of the employees have been there for the long term, though lack contracts. One customer accounts for about 30% of the business. There are a few systems in place, though the business relies on the owner to make sure things get done.

Let's say that due to the previously mentioned factors the business values out at a two multiple. Therefore the business would sell for $175,000 times two = $350,000. This is a before tax number, so the business owner will be left with much less after paying taxes. Is this amount worth the lifetime sweat equity that the owner put into the business?

What if there were contracts on the key employees? What if there were contracts with the largest customers? What if the business ran like a clock without the owner needing to be present? Let's say with these things were in place the multiple could climb to four. Now what would our valuation be?

First off we could have someone with a lower salary run the place, say $50,000. So our calculation would be $200,000 ($250,000 less $50,000) times four or $800,000. We went from $350,000 to $800,000 by doing some simple things over time to make the business better. If we plan our exit correctly, we can also minimize the amount of taxes paid at the sale, increasing our net substantially.

When do you need to start planning your exit from your business? As we stated in the beginning of this book, it is never too early. Start with the Dream, carry it over to your Goals, create and follow a Plan and make sure to do the right Activity every day and you will profit and prosper.

If you did not start with the end in mind, it is never too late to get there. You will most likely need at least three to five years to plan and execute a profitable exit, so for most of you the time to start is now. Seek out an ActionCOACH who can help you get moving in the right direction and can put you in touch with the right group of advisors to make it happen!

Now that we know how to read the Income Statement and Balance Sheet, we need to take a closer look at cash flow, the lifeblood of business.

Review

Do you understand your Balance Sheet and the drivers of value? Knowing the difference between your Current Assets and Current Liabilities and understanding your Current Ratio will help you understand your cash position. Do you have a plan to determine your current business value? Remember it is about growing the value along with growing the profit that will pay off in the long run.

The Balance Sheet ...

A - L = OE

Assets
Liabilities
Owner **E**quity

Measures the financial condition of the business at a certain point in time ...

PART 5

Measuring and Forecasting Cash Flow in Your Business

Cash Flow; some businesses have it, some don't. Most business owners measure their cash flow by constantly monitoring their checkbook. They call people who owe them money in hopes of covering payroll this week. They lay awake in the middle of the night wondering how they can get themselves out of the current situation. Most importantly, they feel great when the check book balance is high, and worry when the balance is low.

Does this sound like you? Do you have a plan for cash that allows you to look into the future with some certainty and tells you when you can pay your bills? Do you have a separate account to keep your profits in? Does your cash collection process mirror the timing of your expenses? What would your business and your life look like if it did?

During this section of the book we will cover information based on past, present and future cash flow from your business. In order to get started we need to discuss the remaining financial report derived from your Chart of Accounts, the Statement of Cash Flows. Just like with the other financial statements we discussed, there are three sections to the Statement of Cash Flows, Cash Flow from Operations, Cash Flow from Investing and Cash Flow from Financing.

The Cash Flow Statement ...

BC + OC + IC + FC = EC

Beginning **C**ash
Operating **C**ash
Investing **C**ash
Financing **C**ash
Ending **C**ash

Measures the financial cash flow of the business over a certain period of time ...

The statement starts and ends with your cash balance from your Balance Sheet based on whatever period you are looking at. Just like your Income Statement or P&L, the Statement of Cash Flows is over a period of time, a month, quarter, or year depending on the use of the statement. If you are looking at a month it will start with the cash balance from last month's Balance Sheet and end with the cash balance from this month's Balance Sheet, same idea for the quarter and year.

Cash Flow from Operations is the money that is generated from the business itself. This section starts with the income generated by the business for the period of time you are looking at. Then adjustments to this income are made if the income is not currently cash. Your Accounts Receivable, Accounts Payable or any other account where your money is hidden or trapped will show as an adjustment to cash.

Let's say for example your company made $30,000 in income over the last month. You can see this profit on your Income Statement. Your Accounts Receivable went up $10,000, Your Accounts Payable dropped $5,000 and you also had $1,000 of depreciation for the month.

Here is what the Cash Flow from Operations section of the statement would look like:

Net Income	$ 30,000
Accounts Receivable	(10,000)
Accounts Payable	(5,000)
Depreciation	1,000
Net Cash Flow from Operation	**$ 16,000**

You can see the business made $30,000 in profit for the month, yet cash only rose by $16,000 for the month based on changes in other parts of the business. Have you ever had a great month in sales and profit and still felt like you were cash poor? Here is the reason why. It is important to understand how the other pieces of your Balance Sheet have an impact on cash so you can do a better job of understanding whether or not there will be more cash available to you in the near future.

The next section of the Statement of Cash Flows has to do with the investment side of your business. This section pertains to any amounts spent or received in conjunction with your long term or fixed assets. If you buy equipment out of cash or sell equipment, the cash proceeds will show up here. For example, let's say you sold an old piece of equipment that had been fully depreciated and bought a new piece of equipment. The old equipment netted you $2,000 and the new piece of equipment cost you $5,000.

Here is how this section of the Statement of Cash Flows would look ...

Equipment Disposed of	$ 2,000
Equipment Purchased	(5,000)
Net Cash Flow from Investing	**$(3,000)**

The last section of the Statement of Cash Flows has to do with financing within the business. This is the section where if there are any loans which have been made, the loan amount and the repayments will show up here along with any funds placed into or taken out of the business by the owner. Continuing along the same example, let's say you borrowed the $5,000 to pay for the equipment along with taking a draw from the business for $5,000 in the month.

Here is how this section would look ...

Loan for Equipment	$ 5,000
Owner's Draw	(5,000)
Net Cash Flow from Financing	**$ 0**

We have covered the three sections of the Statement of Cash Flows and given examples for each section. How does it all fit together? We first need to know the ending Cash balance from the previous month which also represents our beginning balance for this month. Let's say the balance was $5,000. Now we also know the ending balance for the month is also listed on our month end Balance Sheet. We look at that financial report and we see the ending balance is $18,000. We also know the profit for the month is $30,000. Where is the other $17,000?

Beginning Cash Balance	$ 5,000
Net Income	30,000
Accounts Receivable	(10,000)
Accounts Payable	(5,000)
Depreciation	$ 1,000
Net Cash Flow from Operations	16,000
Equipment Disposed of	2,000
Equipment Purchased	(5,000)
Net Cash Flow from Investing	$ (3,000)
Loan for Equipment	5,000
Loan Payment	5,000
Owner's Draw	$ (5,000)
Net Cash Flow from Financing	0
Ending Cash Balance	**$ 18,000**

So where is the other $17,000? $10,000 is owed to us by our customers (Accounts Receivable). We used $5,000 to pay off some suppliers (Accounts Payable). That accounts for $15,000 of the missing money. What about the other $2,000? We used a loan to buy the equipment which was a wash and we took in $2,000 for the old equipment. We are now only missing $4,000. We gave ourselves $5,000 so now we actually have $1,000 too much. Depreciation was $1,000 for the month, so we really never had that cash to begin with. We now have solved the mystery.

Understanding your Statement of Cash Flows can help you identify where your money is trapped, where it went or were it will go. We can expect the $10,000 from Accounts Receivable to show up next month. We also know we will have to make a payment on the equipment. This payment will most likely be far less than $10,000 so we will have some extra cash from the business if we have a similar operational month.

Beginning Cash Balance	$ 18,000
Net Income	30,000
Accounts Receivable	(0)
Accounts Payable	(10,000)
Depreciation	$ (1,000)
Net Cash Flow from Operations	21,000
Equipment Disposed of	1,000
Equipment Purchased	$ (7,000)
Net Cash Flow from Investing	(6,000)
Loan for Equipment	7,000
Loan Payment	500
Owner's Draw	$(30,000)
Net Cash Flow from Financing	(22,500)
Ending Cash Balance	**$ 10,500**

Receivables stayed the same, so there was no impact. We paid down an additional amount against payables because we finally collected the money from the customer to pay our supplier and we took out more money for ourselves since we had a quarterly tax bill due. As the business owner we know all of the decisions we make when it comes to spending or investing money come through us, we sometimes do not know how to keep track of it all. The Statement of Cash Flows is your historical record of your business spending and investment. It tells you exactly where the money went.

A quick review of the Statement of Cash Flows reveals this financial statement also follows the rule of three's. The sections of the Statement, Operating, Investing and Financing all contribute to the addition or subtraction of cash in the business. As an owner, it is important to keep track of your cash. It is also important to be able to forecast where your cash is going to be. That is our next subject. Cash flow Forecasting.

We now know how to track our cash flow, what we need to know next is how to forecast our cash flow. Most business owners can forecast out their cash flow for the next week or two based on where the business is and how much work or revenue is being generated. They start with looking at the Bank balance and then adding in what people owe them, then subtracting out what they need to pay over those next couple of weeks. Sometimes they sleep well at night, other times there is much tossing and turning. Cash flow is usually the number one worry for business owners, yet it is the least measured and understood piece of the business.

Let's look at a simple idea as far as how to get started ...

Checking Account

+ Money In
- Money Out
= Checking Account

Measures the cash flow through the business over a specific period of time ...

Forecasting cash flow can be this easy. The problem lies with knowing what Money In is and what Money Out is. The other problem lies with what time period to forecast. Most large businesses have people dedicated to managing the cash of the business and have the cash flow forecasted out for the next six months to two years. Most business owners do not have someone dedicated to this function, they are doing it themselves. So what is a good time period to start with? The best place to start is somewhere longer than two weeks and shorter than six months.

Here is an example of a forecasting tool which goes out six weeks. Why six weeks? This time period is usually long enough to collect all outstanding receivables and capture the amount of payables for the same time period. It also encompasses at least a month of fixed costs. In addition it makes you the owner look at additional sales needed to cover costs.

6-week Cash Flow Forecast

Date						
Checking Account: *(beginning balance)*						
Additions (+)						
Total Additions (+):						
Subtractions (-)						
Total Subtractions (-):						
Checking Account: *(ending balance)*						

This example starts with establishing a date. Monday's are a good day to forecast your cash flow since most banks are closed on Sunday's. Once we have a date established, we need to find out our checking account balance. We want to use our checking account balance and not our accounting cash balance due to the fact we are looking at cash we have, not adjusted cash.

Once we have our starting balance, we need to know the different ways money can come into the business. There are several ways including invoices paid (Accounts Receivable), cash collections (including credit, debit and checks, all the forms of cash), customer deposits, borrowings, investments and anything else which can put money into the business.

Next we need to know the ways money can leave the business. These would include invoices paid (Accounts Payable), payroll, other fixed expenses, loan payments, taxes and any other way money can go out of the business.

Then we simply create an estimate of how much will come in and go out for the categories we defined for the next week. Start with the beginning balance in your checking account, add in the additions and subtract the subtractions for the week and the remaining amount is what you expect to have in your checking account when the bank closes on Saturday. This will also be the balance you expect to have when the bank opens the following Monday morning. Copy the amount at the bottom of week one to the top of week two.

The first week is usually pretty easy for most business owners. This information is already in their head and putting it into the forecasting tool is not a stretch. Now it starts to get harder. The second week is not as easy to estimate. Knowing what invoices will be paid by customers, knowing what bills need to be paid and the amount of payroll is more difficult to guess. Remember, it is a guess and the only thing you know about your guess is that it is wrong. The only way to get better at something is to practice. The more you work on your Cash Flow Forecast, the easier it gets. It will take time and patience but the end result will be your own peace of mind.

The next step is to drop in your best guess for the second week. You follow the same process to estimate the remaining weeks. This is where it gets tricky. Some of the work you are doing now is going to become a receivable and get paid within this six week timeframe. How do you determine how much will be billed and collected? How do you know what invoices will be created and paid? How do you know what payroll will be six weeks from now?

Here is an example below filled in for a business ...

Date	Week 1	Week 2	Week 3	Week 4	Week 5	Week 6
Checking Account: *(beginning balance)*	30,000	11,750	16,750	8,500	12,250	750
Additions (+)						
Accounts Receivable	5,000	10,000	8,000	7,000	8,000	12,000
Deposits	10,000	8,000	7,000	8,000	12,000	5,000

Date	Week 1	Week 2	Week 3	Week 4	Week 5	Week 6
Cash	500	500	500	500	500	500
Line of Credit			-		2,000	
Total Additions (+):	**15,000**	**18,500**	**15,500**	**15,500**	**22,500**	**17,500**
Subtractions (-)						
Accounts Payable	3,750	4,500	3,750	3,750	8,000	12,000
Fixed Expenses	15,000	6,000	5,000	4,000	15,000	8,000
Payroll	15,000	-	15,000	-	15,000	-
Taxes		3,000		3,000		3,000
Line of Credit				-		2,000
Total Subtractions (-):	33,750	13,500	23,750	10,750	35,000	15,250
Checking Account: *(ending balance)*	11,750	16,750	8,500	13,250	750	3,000

You can see this business expects to grow their cash flow over the next six weeks yet will also need to tap into their line of credit and pay it back. What else do you see? Is this business making or losing money over this time frame? We can see their cash is shrinking, yet it looks like they had their best week in sales in week five.

Now that you know how it works it is time to try this yourself. You will need to gather up some information to get started.

You will need the following items ...

Bank Account Balance *(As of)*
Accounts Receivable Aging Report *(As of)*
Accounts Payable Aging Report *(As of)*
Fixed Costs or Expenses amount and due date per month
Previous payroll reports *(last 2–3)*
Average cash collections by week *(last 2–3)*

As you can see, the bank account balance, the accounts receivable and payable reports should be from the closest date as to when you will create your forecast. As we mentioned before, you will need your opening balance from your checking account as of the Monday you start. You can also run your receivables and payables reports as of that day to create consistency.

Date						
Checking Account: *(beginning balance)*						
Additions (+)						
Total Additions (+):						
Subtractions (-)						
Total Subtractions (-):						
Checking Account: *(ending balance)*						

Step-by-step Instructions:

1. Fill in dates across the top
2. Fill in starting checking account balance
3. Fill in the descriptions of the types of additions and subtractions to cash
4. Estimate the expenses (subtractions) first
5. Add in the additions
6. Calculate ending and beginning cash balances
7. Fine tune the forecast
8. Track the forecast to actual throughout the week
9. Redo the next week by filling in actuals in the first column, adding another column and reforecasting the next six weeks
10. Repeat every week

One of the easiest ways to get started on your forecast is to start with what you know and work toward what you do not know. The best place to start is expenses. You generally know when your payables are due, when your fixed costs or expenses are due, and any other payments that need to be made. Fill in this section first. Remember to take into account outstanding checks which have not cleared the bank. Then when that is completed, fill in the collections area as best you can. Make adjustments to your forecast if the numbers seem to be off.

Fine tune your forecast and keep track of what is happening throughout the week. Repeat the next Monday by first dropping in actuals then reforecasting out the next six weeks. Repeat every week and you will find, with practice, you will get better at forecasting your cash flow and more importantly forecasting your business.

When you make this part of your weekly routine, you will see the benefits almost immediately. You will sleep better at night. You will feel confident in your daily actions. You will have a plan!

Here are a couple of other thoughts when it comes to cash flow forecasting. It is important to have a target balance you would like to see in your checking account. This balance can be based on whatever you think is the best reason. Some business owners like to keep at least one payroll in their account. Others like to keep six months' worth of expenses at hand in case of emergency. You can choose whatever you like, just have a target.

Having a target allows you to move money out of the business when you are consistently above your target. Why would you want to take money out of your business? That is simple; just ask yourself what happens when you have too much money in the business? Do you push as hard to create new sales? Do you spend the money on things the business doesn't really need?

What would happen if you set up a separate profit account? What would happen if you planned to remove this money from the business on the first of the month, just like rent? We discussed treating profit just like a fixed expense in our section on break even. What if you used your cash flow forecaster to take the money away from the business so you actually created profit every month? Would you move closer to your goals and dreams with every profit check?

The last piece of the puzzle when it comes to cash flow is pricing. We discussed pricing in the section on break even within the context of making money. We now need to discuss pricing as it pertains to your cash flow.

Here is an example of a business which has both receivables and payables and the impact it can have on cash flow ...

The Cash Gap ...

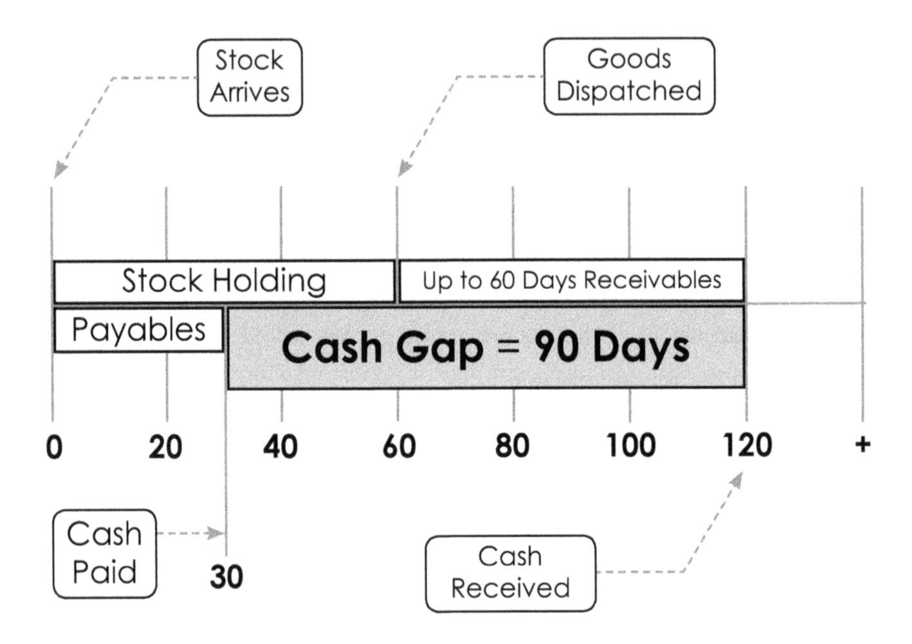

In the example above, the company orders material and eventually uses the material to generate revenue from a customer. The customer is then billed and eventually pays their bill. What matters to you the business owner is the timing of all of these events.

The clock starts ticking on the payable as soon as the stock arrives, sometimes sooner. We usually have 30 days to get this bill paid. We pay the bill 30 days after receiving the goods. We use the materials and bill our customer 60 days after receiving the goods and the customer pays us 60 days later. We paid out cash on day 30 and collected our cash on day 120. We have a 90 day cash gap.

How did we fill this gap? Most business owners fill this gap three ways. We either borrow from our suppliers (using up good will and possibly incurring late fees), use our line of credit (incurring interest expense), or borrowing from our customers. The latter happens when the business owner runs out of the ability to use the first two methods and starts taking deposits on future jobs to pay off the previous job. Which method are you using?

If you are using the first method, are you passing along these charges to your customer? If you are not, what is happening to your Gross Profit Margin %? Your margin will shrink for every extra dollar you have to pay for the supplies. If the customer is also paying late, 60 days instead of 30 days, are you charging them interest to cover your costs? If not, your margin is eroding with each and every day they do not pay.

What can you do to get out of this situation? How much do you need to collect upfront when the customer agrees to the job? What is the ideal amount? Can you collect 100%? How does the customer know what to expect?

Think of all the things you have bought in your life. How did you know when and how to pay for them? Did you ask the checkout person at the grocery store to send you an invoice? Of course not, but how did you know? It starts with your sales person. They are the ones who teach your customers when and how to pay.

Start with what you would like your customers to do. Wouldn't you want all of your money upfront? Are there some businesses that do that? Are you in an industry where it is possible to get all of your money upfront? The key to answering this question lies in the ability of your sales people to ask. The more confidence they have in their ability to sell value, the easier it will be for them to collect money at signing. You can also think of ways to incentivize your sales people like paying commission on collections instead of booked sales. This will align their rewards with your need for cash up front.

Let's look at an example. A remodeling company works with customers on different home projects ranging from small to large. These projects range anywhere from $1,000 to $100,000 with a targeted gross profit of 40%. How much should the sales person ask for as a down payment?

Project Cost	$ 10,000
Materials	(3,000)
Labor	(3,000)
Gross Profit	**$ 4,000**

If the down payment is zero, the business owner will have to come up with the $3,000 for the labor while the project is worked on and possibly have to come up with the $3,000 for materials if the project takes longer than the time given to pay.

If the down payment is 25% or $2,500 the owner still needs to come up with $500 plus materials. If the down payment is 50%, then the labor is taken care of and most of the materials, $5,000 of the $6,000 needed. What is the industry convention? What would the owner like to collect? Obviously 100% is the answer, though many consumers will be hesitant to pay all before they see any work done.

What should the owner target? How about 60%? If the sales person consistently received 60% down with each contract signed, what would that do for cash flow? All of the materials and labor would be taken care of and the remaining payment from the customer is gross profit. No need to borrow from your suppliers and no need to use your line of credit to float your cash. You also get to keep you margin without having it bleed away in finance charges.

Industry convention for remodelers is somewhere between 0 and 50%, so 60% is at the outer boundaries of history. Can consumers be retrained? Maybe. What if you created a plan to retrain your sales staff to collect as much upfront as possible? Would that help with cash flow? Are you paying their commission only when the customer pays? What do you need to change about your collection practices?

What about borrowing from your customers? Collecting all you can upfront is a great way to increase the timing of your cash flow. It is also a way you can get into trouble if you are using this sped up cash flow to pay off old supplier debt. Robbing Peter to pay Paul is one of the ways most businesses get into trouble with their cash. Down payments, not properly applied, can quickly turn into financial heroin. Once you get hooked on using deposits to pay off the last job, it is very difficult to stop.

Just like any other destructive habit, there is really only one way out. Stop It! Simply just stop right now and realize the amount you owe suppliers for previous jobs is really debt. And when you are in debt you need a plan to get out. Call your suppliers and agree to a payment plan for old invoices. Send them money each week, an amount you can handle, until this debt is paid off.

Let them know you will keep current with all new invoices. Fill them in on your plans to grow the business and how important they are to your plan. Let them decide what to do next.

Consistent Cash Flow. Knowing how it is created, how to track it and how to forecast it is one of the most critical pieces to any business. Use this information to learn how for yourself, then when you are ready, teach it to someone else. When you know your cash flows, you know your business.

If you have read this far and have not done your cash flow forecast, stop reading and go back and do it now. When you are comfortable with how to do it, you are ready to take the next financial step in your business, budgeting and forecasting profit.

Review

Do you know how to read your Cash Flow Statement? Do you know what it tells you?

The Cash Flow Statement ...

BC + OC + IC + FC = EC

Beginning **C**ash
Operating **C**ash
Investing **C**ash
Financing **C**ash
Ending **C**ash

Measures the financial cash flow of the business over a certain period of time ...

Do you know where your cash is? Do you have sound cash management strategies in place to maximize your return on your money? Collection practices?

Checking Account

+ Money In

- Money Out

= Checking Account

Measures the cash flow through the business over a specific period of time ...

Do you know how much cash your business will need or generate for you? Are you prepared for week to week variations in cash flow? This is an area of your business that you will need to put aside time every week to work on. Do you have time set aside in your calendar to work on the financial side of the business?

PART 6

Budgeting and Forecasting — How to make it work for you

We have discussed how important it is to track your financial information on a regular basis through reading your Income Statement, Balance Sheet and Statement of Cash Flows. Understanding where you are is an essential component to being able to understand where you are going. Budgeting and Forecasting are an integral component into looking out into the future and deciding your path.

We have discussed the importance of forecasting out your cash flow in your business in order to better understand you cash flow needs and changes. That is just one component of your business. What about marketing, sales, work flow and resource management? These things are essential to understanding the path you are on.

Early in this book we discussed the idea of dreams. Turning your dreams into solid goals that you have a chance of reaching is part of the function of being a business owner. No one else will take the time to look out into the future to determine why to grow the business and by how much. Only you the owner can do that.

The first step of this process is looking out past one year to decide where you would like the business to go. A good starting point most business owners can accomplish is to create five year goals. Why five years? Looking five years out in your business gets rid of any seasonality, short term business challenges and anything else that clouds your ability to see the horizon of the business world.

You are the captain of your ship, and the most important duty the captain has on any vessel is to make sure the ship is on course. A five year goal can become the fixed point for the vessel to sail towards as it handles the day to day challenges of operating on the high seas of business.

What are some things to look at as you create your five year plan? Here is a list of questions you will need to answer before creating a financial template. At this point take some time to answer each question to the best of your ability and answer each question as if you are looking at your business five years from today. Remember, the more detail and clarity, the better the answer.

5-year Business Vision Questions ...

How big is your business? # of clients, annual revenue, annual profit being generated, your income ... What is the value of your business at this point and time? And why would someone else want to buy your business?

On a physical level, what does your business look like? Where is your business located, Do you have multiple locations?

What does your organization in your business look like? How many employees do you have? What roles do they play? Do you have additional partners/ jr. partners? What role do you play in the business? How many hours are you working? How many days are you working? What are some common traits and characteristics of your employees? What is the culture of your business like?

Who is your target market? Depict your ideal clients. Why does a client rave about your business? How are you perceived in the business community?

Why is your business different for from all your competition, what makes you unique? What makes you the best at what you do? What products and services do you offer and at what prices/fees? What type of customer service do you offer?

What functional areas of your business are systematized with processes and procedures? Be specific.

How do you market your business, what are the primary methods/strategies you use to market your practice? What percentage of your new customers comes from client referrals? How do you insure that your clients provide referrals? Where else do you receive referrals? What types of businesses do you partner with for referrals? Are there any businesses you have strategic alliances with?

What areas of your business are outsourced?

What is your exit strategy? Are you selling to new owners, existing partners? How much will you sell it for? Will you leverage your business to create passive income?

....

....

....

....

....

Difficult questions to answer, aren't they? What was the easiest section for you to cover? What section was the most difficult for you to work through? As you can see, there are many variables in your business that you need to have an idea or a plan around. Having a general understanding around each one of these questions will allow you and the business to put together some meaningful financial goals for the team to achieve.

This is what is referred to as a Strategic Plan ...

Dreams x **Goals** x **Plan** x **Activity**

Once you have this strategic plan, it is now time to lay out some meaningful goals, create a plan and corresponding activity and create a culture of accountability to measure and maximize activity based results for the next year. This is the purpose of a budget. The next step in our process is to give you the business owner some tools you can use to put together your budget.

We are actually going to use the information we discussed when deriving your Break Even for your business. By breaking the business down into the components of Revenue, Gross Profit Margin % and Fixed Costs we can get going on a high level budget right away.

Here is how it would look ...

	Next Year
1. **Revenue**	
2. **Gross Profit Margin %**	
3. **Gross Profit** *(1 times 2)*	
4. **Fixed Expenses**	
5. **Profit** *(3 less 4)*	

Start with the amount of Revenue you think you can produce next year. Take the Gross Profit Margin % you came up with from the Break Even calculator and drop it into the schedule above. . Add in the projected fixed costs for the year. Calculate the amount of profit you will create. What does that number look like?

Let's work through an example. Let's say we want to produce $400,000 of revenue in our business next year. We have fixed costs of $10,000 per month and our Gross Profit Margin % is 40%.

Here is what our budget would look like ...

	Next Year
1. **Revenue**	$ 400,000
2. **Gross Profit Margin %**	40%
3. **Gross Profit** *(1 times 2)*	160,000
4. **Fixed Expenses**	120,000
5. **Profit** *(3 less 4)*	**$ 40,000**

The first question would be where did the $400,000 number come from? In this case the business owner was able to produce $375,000 of revenue in the previous year, so $400,000 sounded like a good achievable goal. This is referred to as linear thinking. Linear thinking is taking the past and projecting it out incrementally to determine the future. There is no basis for this thinking to be considered better than other methods except in its ease of use.

Is $40,000 enough profit for you or the business? At 10% of revenue (40,000/400,000) this is a fairly decent net profit percentage. Would you be happy with 10%? Some business owners would be ecstatic, others would be unhappy. It is all up to you. What if you decided that $40,000 is not enough? What can you do about it?

Start with the amount of profit you would like to make next year. This number should be based on your monetary needs and also be based on your strategic plan. What is the money for?

Write out a list of the money needs for you and the business next year ...

....

....

....

....

....

Is there a debt repayment plan in place? Do you need money to buy something or go somewhere based on your dreams? What about investments back into the business? Do you have money set aside to grow through marketing and sales?

Once you have determined how much profit you need, how much will have to be paid in taxes? Add that amount to your profit. Add in the projected fixed costs for the year. Take the Gross Profit Margin % you came up with from the Break Even calculator and drop it into the schedule above. Calculate the amount of revenue you will need to produce. What does that number look like?

Let's work through an example. Let's say we want to make $100,000 of profit in our business instead of $40,000 next year. We have still have the same fixed costs of $10,000 per month and our Gross Profit Margin % is still 40%.

Here is what our budget would look like ...

	Next Year
1. **Revenue**	$ 550,000
2. **Gross Profit Margin %**	40%
3. **Gross Profit** *(1 times 2)*	220,000
4. **Fixed Expenses**	120,000
5. **Profit** *(3 less 4)*	**$ 100,000**

We would need to produce $550,000 of revenue at our 40% GPM% instead of $400,000. That is $150,000 more of revenue or 35%. Which plan is better, the one that gives you a result or the one that creates the result you need? This is the difference between top down and bottom up budgeting.

Another way to say this would be it is the difference between linear thinking and fractal thinking. The past does not dictate your future, only you can do that. Fractal thinking is based on what you think is possible at this moment without the anchors of the past. Think of all of the mistakes you have made as a business owner. How much did those mistakes cost you in terms of lost revenue and profit? How much better off will your revenue and profits be because of those mistakes?

Fractal thinking is taking the learning's from those mistakes and turning them into a larger and more profitable business for you. What if you decided it was time to double your business?

What would that look like ... ?

	Next Year
1. **Revenue**	$ 750,000
2. **Gross Profit Margin %**	40%
3. **Gross Profit** *(1 times 2)*	300,000
4. **Fixed Expenses**	120,000
5. **Profit** *(3 less 4)*	**$ 180,000**

You just took your $375,000 revenue company and doubled it and made yourself an extra $140,000 in profit for the next year. The little voice inside your head is probably saying "that's not possible." Why not? What are the limits or barriers to your growth? What if the little voice in your head is the biggest barrier you have?

Take a step back and ask yourself, what would it take to double my business? The most interesting thing about this exercise is that it takes the same amount of time and brain space to think big as it does to think small. What areas of your business do you find yourself thinking small? How big is your market? How much of your market do you currently service? What is the maximum market share you could possess?

How many people do you need to help? That is the ultimate question when it comes to growing your business. If the answer is not many then your business will most likely stay small. If the answer is everyone then the business has to grow. Why would you deny the marketplace your services if you truly believe in them?

It is time for you to write down your goals for next year. In the blank sheet below, ask yourself how much revenue you need to produce to help the number of people you need to help and at what profit margin. Add in the amount of fixed costs or capacity you will need to find and support that many customers, then calculate your profit. Does it fit with what you had in mind? If not, redo until it does.

	Next Year
1. **Revenue**	
2. **Gross Profit Margin %**	
3. **Gross Profit** *(1 times 2)*	
4. **Fixed Expenses**	
5. **Profit** *(3 less 4)*	

What do you think? Do you know how to make this budget happen? If so, it is most likely still in your comfort zone and it will not push you to learn and grow. If not, and you are uncomfortable with the numbers and do not yet know how to make it happen, then you will most certainly grow as an owner and a person. There is only one thing that you know at this point, the final result will not be what you wrote down. Be comfortable with being wrong because you can always fix it!

Once you have decided on your numbers, it is now time to get the rest of the team involved. If your team is big enough, you have most likely involved them already. If not, then they need to know the goals and what they will be held accountable for.

The revenue budget needs to be broken down into the business lines then to the sales people involved in those business lines. A pricing plan needs to be created to ensure that the Gross Profit Margin that is in the budget can be achieved. The fixed costs need to be assigned to allow you the owner to delegate decisions on investing and spending.

Each of these areas is most likely going to need more detail to create some clarity and focus on the true financial drivers of your business. We already discussed breaking down revenue and pricing. What about fixed costs? These need to be broken down into the major categories and assigned to the team or yourself so you only spend what you indicated was available for that item. It is easier to spend less when you know there is a limit!

The budget is the tool to make sure everyone understands their role in the profitability of the company. It also allows the business to measure the effectiveness of those roles and potentially reward the team when goals are met and exceeded.

As we mentioned before, it is better to have variable costs than fixed costs in a business. Making some of the team pay variable based on the outcome of the business compared to budget allows for the win-win when it comes to compensation. When the business exceeds baseline profitability, there is more money to share with the team.

As a business owner, you take the risk. This risk needs a return on investment. Once that return is met, then the extra return can be split by the business and the team. Setting a budget and determining the appropriate rate of return on your investment will allow you to give the team a way for everyone to make more.

This may take some time to do as most employees are employees because they like the stability of a paycheck. Most are also looking for ways to increase their pay, and would like that pay to be additional salary. This will increase your fixed costs, making the business more vulnerable when there are sharp fluctuations in demand. By sharing this risk there is a buy in to share short term pain and long term gain.

Once your budget is finalized and the team has been engaged in their part, the next step is to put it in place. All monthly financial information should be analyzed versus the budget to determine if the business is on or off track. Each area that has been assigned a portion of the budget to produce or manage should be scored against this foundation.

Once the budget is put in place and there is a focus on actual compared to budget, the question that needs to be addressed is if you are behind what will you need to do to catch up and if you are ahead what do you need to do to stay ahead? By comparing the business back to the budget you can determine where you need more attention.

You will also need to start forecasting, which in essence is the creation of a short term budget. A monthly process you can use at this point is to compare actual versus budget then forecast out the next three months. If you are ahead, how can you stay ahead, if you are behind how can you catch up. The first attempts at a budget may be difficult at first, just like your cash flow forecasting. Keep working at it, with practice you will get better and better with every attempt.

We now have the first two pieces of our formula covered. Dreams and Goals. We now need to develop a plan to achieve the budgetary goal and then determine the best activity to build into the plan and hold the team accountable to. The next part of this book is devoted to this topic.

Review

The budget process we discussed earlier is a good start. What additional line items do you and your business need to focus on and how much input from the team do you need to create a long term strategic plan for your business? There a remany tools out there to choose from, the most important step is getting started.

PART 7

KPI's and the 5 Ways — How to Create a Business Dashboard

As we have mentioned many times in this book, the financials are the result or scorecard of your business. They let you know if you are on track or off track when it comes to your goals and dreams. They also tell you where you need to focus if an area is off track. What they do not tell you is how to make it happen.

The plan or how to accomplish your goals is one of the most important aspects of running a business. Plans need to be written down, shared with the team and followed on a continuous basis in order to have a chance of reaching your goals. Without a plan a dream or goal is just a wish.

So how do you develop a plan? Well, first you need to understand what the goal is. Are you clear as far as the goal is concerned? The tighter the target, the easier it is to focus. Focus, or Follow One Course Until Successful, will allow you to achieve your goals through a well thought out plan.

So what goes into a plan? Let's start with what plan you are creating. Every year you will need to update and review your strategic plan along with the creation of the plan and budget for the coming year. This should take the business about two days to accomplish. Many companies will do this at an offsite where the distractions are minimal so as to be able to completely focus. There is also an element of team bonding that goes into this process.

Once the annual plan is completed this plan should be reviewed every 90 days to ensure the company stays on track, preferably with a one day event that is also conducted offsite. Once a month for at least half a day the results of the month should be analyzed and every week business areas need to review progress towards the goal. Calendars should be reviewed daily to keep focus on the task or tasks at hand.

Does your business take this much time to plan on a regular basis? Most business owners do not take the time to plan because they are busy getting other things done. They are mired in the detail and are stressed and tired on a daily basis because they see their dreams slowly slipping away. Simply put, you must slow down to speed up. If you are not following the recommended amount of planning time listed above, you are most likely not achieving your goals.

So what areas of your business need a plan? The first thing you are going to need is a dashboard. What is a dashboard you ask? Imagine getting into a dump truck and seeing all sorts of levers and buttons. What if they did not have labels? What if you had to test each one of them to determine exactly what they do?

You find that one lever lifts the bucket up and down. Another moves the truck forward and another moves it in reverse. Another lever changes the level of the bucket and you also find out that the two gauges are for oil pressure and the gas tank. You find these things out through trial and error and label each gauge and lever as you discover their true purpose.

This is just like a business. Your dashboard consists of the things that move your business forward, backward, up and down. Sometimes you have to try many things to find the right ones that work. This is what a dashboard helps you do, find the right things that work and keep doing them until they do not work anymore.

Let's start with looking at a possible dashboard that you could use in your business to keep track of your vital statistics.

Let's start with the 5 ways model as shown on the opposite page ...

5 WAYS BUSINESS CHASSIS

Number of Leads

x

Conversion Rate

=

Customers

x

# of Transactions

x

Average $$$ Sale

=

Revenue

x

Profit Margins

=

Profit

There are three outputs and five inputs into any business. The outputs are Customers, Revenue and Profit. The inputs, or the 5 ways, are Leads, Conversion Rate, # of Transactions, Avg. $$$ Sale and Profit Margins.

As you can see, we have already invested most of this book into helping you to determine the last three parts of this formula, Revenue x Profit Margins = Profit. This is exactly the information you used to create your own budget. What the rest of the 5 ways model allows you to do is create a dashboard that allows you to achieve your budgeted revenue.

What we need to do next is expand this budget sheet to include the rest of the 5 ways model.

It would look something like this ...

	Next Year
1. **Leads**	
2. **Conversion Rate**	
3. **Customers** *(1 times 2)*	
4. **# of Transactions**	
5. **Average $$$ Sale**	
6. **Revenue** *(3 times 4 times 5)*	
7. **Gross Profit Margin %**	
8. **Gross Profit** *(6 times 7)*	
9. **Fixed Expenses**	
10. **Profit** *(8 less 9)*	

So let's go back to our example business that was producing $750,000 in revenue and $180,000 in profit. Let's also assume the company has a 25% conversion rate on new prospects and an average dollar sale of $2,500, meaning that each time a customer buys from us they buy on average $2,500 worth of stuff. They also on average buy from us twice a year.

Here is what that business would look like ...

	Next Year
1. **Leads**	600
2. **Conversion Rate**	25%
3. **Customers** *(1 times 2)*	150
4. **# of Transactions**	2.00
5. **Average $$$ Sale**	2,500
6. **Revenue** *(3 times 4 times 5)*	$ 750,000
7. **Gross Profit Margin %**	40%
8. **Gross Profit** *(6 times 7)*	300,000
9. **Fixed Expenses**	120,000
10. **Profit** *(8 less 9)*	**$ 180,000**

At a 25% conversion rate this company would need 600 leads to get 150 customers who would buy $2,500 worth of stuff twice a year. This would gross $750,000 in revenue and at a 40% Gross Profit Margin net $300,000 in gross profit less our $120,000 of fixed expenses would yield a $180,000 net profit.

So as we look at this business, in what areas are we going to need a plan? What line items are inputs and what line items are outputs? Let's start at the top. Leads. Where do leads come from? Would it be fair to say that leads are produced as a result of our marketing efforts? Are we going to need a plan to produce 600 leads next year?

Conversion rate? Are we going to need a sales plan to convert these leads into customers? Number of transactions. How are we going to get our customers to buy form us twice a year? Avg. $$$ Sale. Do we need a plan to make sure our average sale is $2,500?

Looking at our chart above, what would happen if we decide we need a plan to increase each of the 5 ways? Let's look at what the impact would be of changing these inputs into the business by just 10%.

Here are the new results ...

	Next Year
1. **Leads**	660
2. **Conversion Rate**	28%
3. **Customers** *(1 times 2)*	182
4. **# of Transactions**	2.20
5. **Average $$$ Sale**	2,750
6. **Revenue** *(3 times 4 times 5)*	$ 1,098,075
7. **Gross Profit Margin %**	44%
8. **Gross Profit** *(6 times 7)*	483,153
9. **Fixed Expenses**	150,000
10. **Profit** *(8 less 9)*	**$ 333,153**

You can see we have a tremendous increase in Revenue (+46%) and a huge increase in Gross Profit (+61%). You can also see we added some fixed costs or capacity to handle the additional work and our profit still registers a large increase. This is the power of measurement and management.

The ability to significantly increase the size and profitability of your business doesn't hinge on your ability to dramatically reshape your business but on your ability to measure and create small consistent incremental increases in the various parts of your business. Think about the power of that and how you can finally start making the money you know you deserve.

As you look at the model above, we need a plan around numbers 1, 2, 4, 5, 7, and 9. Each of these pieces of the business has a very clear goal and can be measured to determine if the business is on or off track. In order to measure each of these pieces of the business, we are going to have to determine what and how we will measure for each line item.

Here is what a dashboard would look like including all of the above line items ...

The Business Dashboard ...

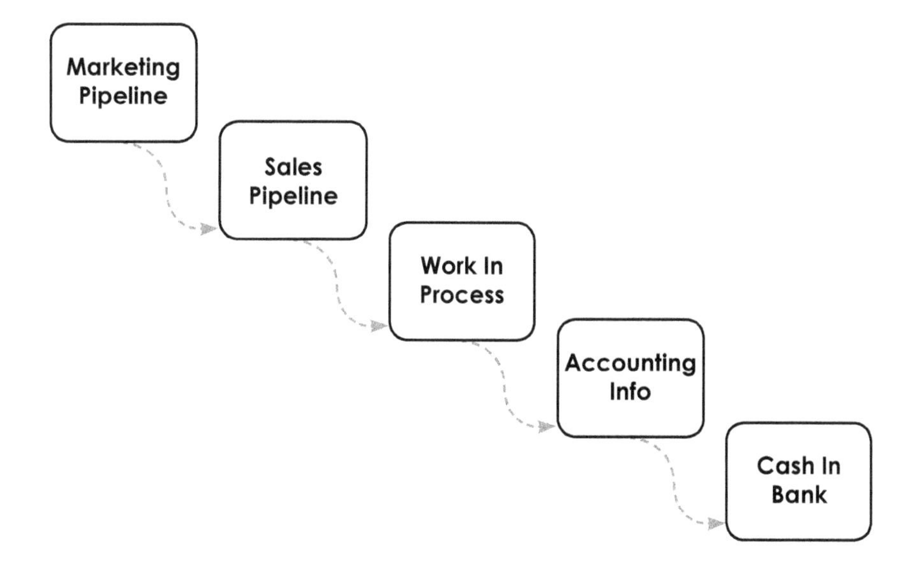

Your Marketing Pipeline report would include all of your activity needed to be able to generate leads at a predetermined cost per lead. The Marketing Plan would be measured by the Marketing Pipeline.

The Sales Pipeline report would include all of the activity necessary to close the leads provided by the Marketing Plan. This report would measure the effectiveness of the business and the sales team in closing ability.

The Work in Process report would capture all of the information necessary to ensure that Gross Margins the work was sold at are actually realized. This report will also help with resource utilization as the work is getting done.

We have already invested much time in discussing the Accounting Information. This is where all of the data concerning financial results is stored. Cash in Bank is the ultimate goal. How much money you have and will have in your checking account is the result of all of the other activities.

So where do the line items from the 5 Ways report fit into the Dashboard? The Marketing Pipeline report will tell us if we are on track to achieve our 600 leads (Line 1). This pipeline report will also give us our return on investment numbers for our Marketing Plan along with the most profitable lead generation strategies.

The Marketing Pipeline will also let us know how many leads are in the system and what resources we need to allocate to the sales force to properly work the leads. In a sense, the Marketing Pipeline feeds the Sales Pipeline as shown by the arrow in the chart.

The Sales Pipeline will help us to track and measure our Conversion Rate (Line 2). The overall Conversion Rate is just one part of the pipeline. There are usually many steps in a sales process and each of these steps can be another conversion measurement. The Sales Pipeline will also measure effectiveness by lead source, sales person, Gross Margin at Sale (Line 7) and a host of other sorts on the data. The Sales Pipeline feeds directly into the Work in Process Pipeline.

The Work in Process Pipeline allows the company to measure the productivity of the workforce and also will be part of measuring the Gross Margin (Line 7). The work is sold at a certain margin, though that margin is not always realized by the production team. Production can be measured by job, by employee, by business line and other possible sorts. The Work in Process Pipeline feeds directly into the Accounting System.

The Accounting System is the place where most of the other line items are measured. Number of Transactions (Line 4) and Avg. $$$ Sale (Line 5) can easily be found in your accounting data. These line items can also be found in your other previous pipelines if measured properly.

The Accounting Data flows directly into Cash Measurement. The point of measuring all of the other aspects of the business is to allow you the business owner to be able to produce consistent cash flow results from your business. If there is not enough cash generated to keep the business going you can easily pinpoint the source of the problem or problems and work to correct them.

The Dashboard actually then looks like this ...

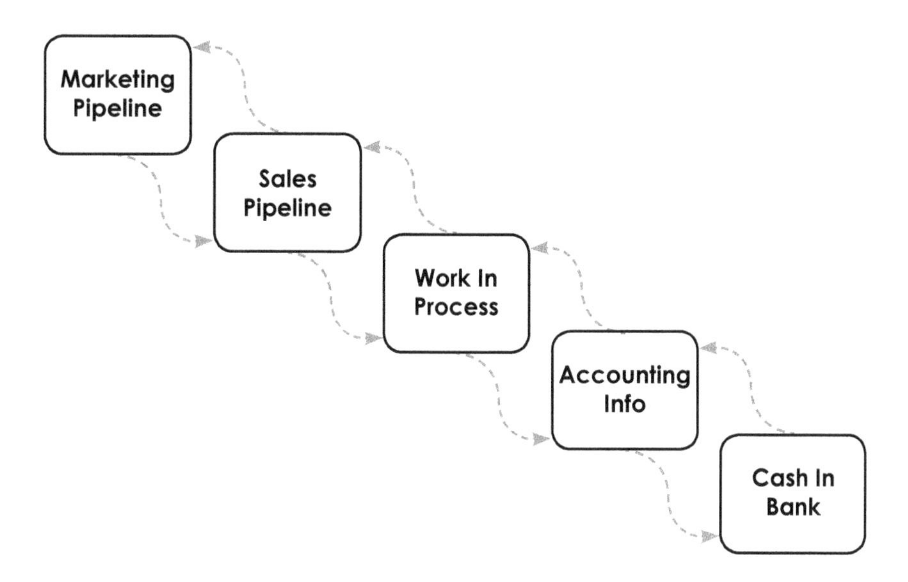

Think of it this way, what are the things a business owner can do if there is not enough cash forecasted in the bank in the near term? The first place to go would be the Accounting Info – Accounts Receivable and Line of Credit. The next place to go would be progress payments of job completion payments out of the Work in Process section.

The next logical place would be the Sales Pipeline and possible down payments on new work. The last place to look for more money would be the Marketing budget. All of these are areas where either cash can be generated or saved.

The most interesting thing about this progression is that it is the opposite of what most business owners do when cash is low. Slash the Marketing Budget, skinny down the Sales Team and cut production staff when in a crisis is the norm. All of these things make the situation worse rather than better. These decisions actually choke off future cash flow just when it is needed most, keeping the business in a downward spiral until there is some outside cash infusion or crash.

What if you decided to invest in Sales Training, stop selling lower margin items and focus better on your target market? What would these things do to your bottom line? Let's go back to our original business to get some answers.

	Next Year
1. **Leads**	300
2. **Conversion Rate**	40%
3. **Customers** *(1 times 2)*	120
4. **# of Transactions**	2.00
5. **Average $$$ Sale**	2,500
6. **Revenue** *(3 times 4 times 5)*	$ 600,000
7. **Gross Profit Margin %**	50%
8. **Gross Profit** *(6 times 7)*	300,000
9. **Fixed Expenses**	120,000
10. **Profit** *(8 less 9)*	**$ 180,000**

As you can see, we need to generate half as many leads to get the same amount of profit from the business. Bigger is not always better when it comes to Revenue. By bumping our Gross Profit Margin from 40 to 50% by discontinuing lower profit items and increasing our conversion rate from 25 to 40% through sales training and better lead qualification, the results are staggering.

Results like these are only available to businesses that know their numbers. By measuring the essential elements we are able to create Key Performance Indicators (KPI's) that drive focus and results.

So let's take a look at our Dashboard again ...

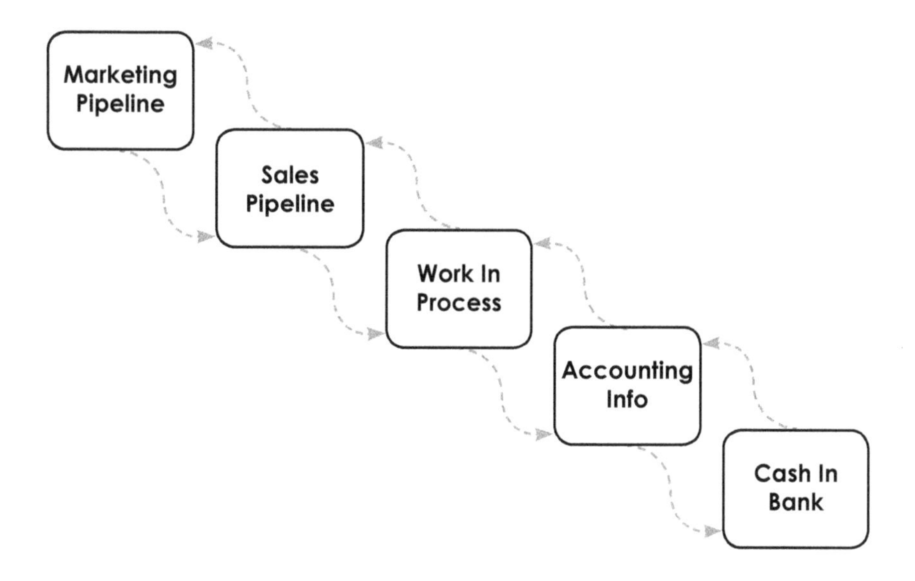

Think back to our Dreams x Goals x Plan x Activity. The dreams are used to create the goals, the goals are used to create the plan and the plan is used to create the correct activity. Alignment. Alignment in focus and alignment in results.

For each of the areas listed above, we are going to need some KPI's that are related to activity. We need to focus on Activity in order to achieve the results we need to get. Remember-activity is assigned, results are generated. Let me say that one more time. Activity is assigned, results are generated. If we are looking to achieve results, then we must assign responsibility for each of the areas of activity we need to grow our business.

For the Marketing Pipeline we are going to need to hold someone responsible for results. The Marketing Pipeline report will allow everyone in the organization to see if the activity needed to generate results is occurring on a consistent basis.

Some typical KPI's in most Marketing Plans would be number of marketing strategies used, acceptable cost per lead, leads generated per day/week/month and quality of lead within target market. By successfully focusing on the activity, the Marketing Pipeline can become a predictor of future business.

The Sales Pipeline KPI's are typically focused on interactions with prospects that lead to sales. Depending on the type of business and size of sale, the sales process can be broken down and measured by small incremental steps of activity that allow the customer to make the buying decision. Number of phone calls, meetings, proposals and quotes will generally be the focus of the activity for this section of the business. Other important information that can be gathered from the Sales Pipeline pertains to sales cycle time and potential Avg. $$$ Sale and Gross Margin.

The closer the prospect gets to a buying decision the higher the probability of buying. Therefore the pipeline can be probability weighted and sales and margin can actually be forecast as a result of the record keeping in the Sales Pipeline. The Key Performance Indicators can actually become Key Predictive Indicators.

The Work in Process Pipeline report is the key to profitability in your business. Activity measured here can range from Total Billable Hours to Job Costing by project depending on the business type. For some businesses it may be Inventory turns or labor cost per sale. By focusing on the correct activity in this section, profitability will follow.

The Work in Process information feeds directly into the Accounting machine. There are many different possible KPI's in the Accounting world as you have already seen. The trick is to find the ones that are most meaningful to your business and make sure the focus stays on them.

All of this then feeds into the Cash Flow forecast and allows the owner to properly handle the lifeblood of the business. By having all of this information at your fingertips you can now know with some certainty where improvements are necessary and where investments can be made to achieve the highest possible Return on Investment.

The last piece of the puzzle is making sure that someone is responsible and held accountable for the results of each of the business functions. The Marketing Director will need to develop a plan of activity that will produce said marketing results. The Sales Manager will be responsible for holding their sales people accountable to the correct daily activity to achieve results.

The Production Manager is responsible for profitability and the Finance Manager is responsible for gathering all of the correct information, correct billings and collections. This results in solid long term cash flow growth that can be used to grow the business.

There are two other parts of your business that need to be measured and managed within these components that we have yet to discuss. One of them is Customer Satisfaction. Measuring and managing the customer expectations and experience is a vital component to any business. The trick is to find a way to empirically measure the experience and make sure there are KPI's in place to manage the activity associated with delivering this experience.

Customer Satisfaction can be assigned to any box, though it most likely fits best in the Work in Process area. Make sure there are clear measurements and goals assigned to the team to keep the focus on the customer and not just the numbers. Sometimes these two can compete and there needs to be a way for the team to understand how to deliver customer satisfaction and profitability.

Team Satisfaction is the other component of your business that needs attention. It can be easy to take the team for granted until the top performers realize this and move on. By keeping the pulse of the team you the owner can get better feedback and make sure there is the highest level of satisfaction possible.

The Finance area is most likely the best place to handle this as this is normally a human resource function. Once again this is an area than can compete with profitability but can also compete with customer satisfaction.

Think of the goal as a three legged stool. Profitability, Customer Satisfaction and Team Satisfaction all need to be consistently improved as to create solid ongoing business structure. Keeping the focus on all three will allow you the owner to make sure there is activity assigned to each of these.

Dreams x Goals x Plan x Activity. Daily Activity. That is the key to creating a consistently profitable business that someday can work without you. When will you put your Dashboard into place and assign responsibility for activity to generate the results you need?

PART 8

Next Steps

What areas of your business are working well and what areas need the most improvement?

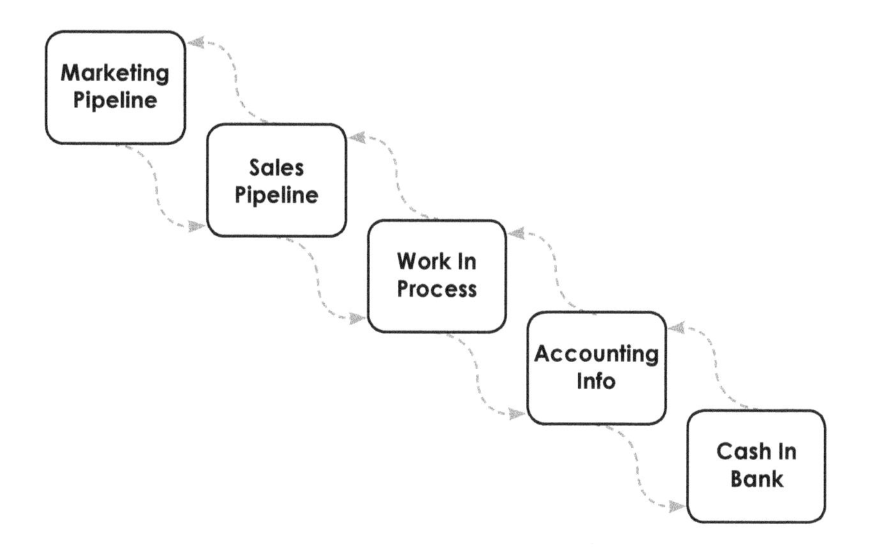

Developing Key Performance or Key Predictive Indicators for each one of the above items should be one of the first steps on your list to creating consistent cash flow. Creating, assigning, then holding the team accountable to the distinct areas of activity will make everyone's position easier and will make the consistent and permanent removal of all excuses possible.

WThe next part is up to you. You can put this book down and go back to what you were doing or you can page back to the exercises and complete them to the best of your ability. You can then start to implement the changes necessary in your business to make fundamental improvements and have consistent cash flow.

If you are ready to get going, here is a simple 13 point plan to get you started ...

1. **Get your numbers up to date** — you cannot start making changes until you know precisely where you are. Work with your Accountant to properly set up your chart of accounts and your financial statements.
2. **Review your Scorecard with your Accountant** — make sure you have an accurate starting point so that you will be able to measure the effectiveness of your changes.
3. **Examine your Money Beliefs** — know why money does not appear for you and some of your self-sabotage methods and work to change them.
4. **Calculate your Break Even** — understand each of your Break Even measure (BE1, BE2 and BE3) so you know exactly how much revenue and at what margin you need to cover all of your expenses including profit.
5. **Create a Cash Flow Forecast** — understanding what will be in your checking account will automatically start you down the road to consistent growth and less stress over money.
6. **Create a Budget** — As the owner, you must set the course for the business for the next year. Outline the financial goals of the company and get the team involved. Accountability and Results will follow.
7. **Start Forecasting** — when things do not work out as planned, which is often the case, be ready to shift gears and create a new plan to get back on course.
8. **Create your Business Dashboard** — look at each of the main drivers of your business and begin to measure the most important and vital components of each one. Marketing, Sales, Work Flow, Financials and Cash Flow each need focused activity to produce results.

9. **Customer and Team** — Make sure there is a focus on these additional components of the business on a daily basis. It will make growth easier in the long run.
10. **Daily and Weekly Accountability** — look at your dashboard each day to determine if the activity is happening that will produce results. Meet with the team weekly to keep the focus on activity and not on excuses.
11. **Know where the Money goes** — Have a plan for profit. Know exactly why you need it and what you will use it for and it will appear.
12. **Work on your Leadership Skills** — you now have a built in system of accountability. Use it and keep the focus where it needs to be. Always keep an eye out for new talent; you will need it as you grow.
13. **Demand Results** — if results do not happen, make changes. Some of your team will thrive, some will survive and some will not make it. Some of your team will need to move on, make it easy for them to do so.

This list will not be easy but I can guarantee that it will be worth it. By knowing if your business is getting the right things done on a daily basis make owning a business much more fun and rewarding. Keep the focus on the team and let them take care of the customers and the business will take care of you.

The Cycle of Business ...

By implementing this "System of Accountability," the assessment of each team member is based on numbers not just gut feel. Healthy competition amongst team members fosters growth by focusing on personal bests and team milestones. Pay for performance is easier to implement because the results are verifiable.

The team is happier because they know their responsibilities and are held accountable to them. You no longer feel compelled to be involved in each and every detail because you can monitor the activity and results from afar.

The team can take care of the customers because they know the dynamic tension between profitability and customer service. Decisions can be made quickly or remade if things are not working as intended. The impact of these decisions is owned by the team and therefore personal responsibility can be taken.

The customers will receive better service and results, and therefore are much more likely to refer their network back to your business. It is far less expensive to keep customers happy than to go get new ones and the referrals are like icing on the cake.

You now have a way to run your business without you and keep you finger on the daily pulse from anywhere you like. Alignment. Alignment to your dreams and goals is possible. You just need to take action.

D x **G** x **P** x **A**

Dreams x Goals x Plan x Activity

Here is a checklist of the items we have discussed in this book along with a space for you to commit to a timeline. Fill in the checklist and be realistic about your timeline. Determine where you need the most assistance and fill in the names of people you need to contact for help.

Task	Start Date	Completion Date	Assistance
1. DxGxPxA Score			
2. Get your numbers up to date			
3. Review your Scorecard with your Accountant			
4. Examine your Money Beliefs			

Task	Start Date	Completion Date	Assistance
5. Calculate your Break	....	....	....
6. Create a Cash Flow Forecast	....	....	....
7. Create a Budget	....	....	....
8. Start Forecasting	....	....	....
9. Create your Business Dashboard	....	....	....
10. Customer and Team Satisfaction	....	....	....
11. Daily and Weekly Accountability	....	....	....
12. Know where the Money goes	....	....	....
13. Work on your Leadership Skills	....	....	....
14. Demand Results	....	....	....
15. New DxGxPxA Score	....	....	....

Start by changing yourself and your daily activity and the rest will fall in line over time. Time to get into Action!

ABOUT THE AUTHOR

Tom Palzewicz

After serving in the Armed Services on the USS Scamp, a nuclear submarine, Tom ventured into the world of accounting and finance, receiving his Bachelor of Business Administration degree with a major in Accounting. He enjoyed a rewarding career in banking with Firstar, Marshall & Ilsley, Associated Bank and US Bank. While working in corporate banking Tom discovered his passion lay in a much different arena – community growth and development. He immediately recognized ActionCOACH would help him to achieve this vision.

Tom became a certified ActionCOACH business coach in 2005. His 15+ years in finance, management and team-building provide a solid foundation of expertise for business management and improvement. He extends these talents to aid in job creation for his business clients to succeed and grow by adding new employees, thereby contributing to the economic stability and quality of life in Southeast Wisconsin.

Tom is generous with his time, coaching non-profit organizations pro bono to help them make a more meaningful difference to people in need in our community. Tom is an elite Platinum level Business Coach, consistently ranking as a "Top 100" ActionCOACH Business Coach in the world. A native of Milwaukee, Tom currently resides in Brookfield, Wisconsin, with his wife, three children and family dog.

Lightning Source UK Ltd.
Milton Keynes UK
UKHW021833110619
344249UK00020B/437/P